THE ELEMENTS OF ZEN

David Scott is an internationally known writer specializing in Japan, health and cookery. He has written a number of highly successful cookery titles including *The Demi-veg Cookbook* and *Japanese Cooking*, a book on Japanese life and culture entitled *Samurai and Cherry Blossom* and *The Essential Guide to Japan*. He co-authored *The Fighting Arts* – a guide to the martial arts – and founded the Liverpool Uechi-Ryu karate club. He is a fifth Dan.

David Scott studies Zen under the guidance of Genpo Merzel Sensei. He lives in Liverpool and is co-owner of the Everyman Bistro.

Tony Doubleday is a long-standing member of the Kanzoan Sangha (a Zen Buddhist Community) and a student of Genpo Merzel Sensei. He lives in Exeter and works as a solicitor.

The *Elements Of* is a series designed to present high quality introductions to a broad range of essential subjects.

The books are commissioned specifically from experts in their fields. They provide readable and often unique views of the various topics covered, and are therefore of interest both to those who have some knowledge of the subject, as well as those who are approaching it for the first time.

Many of these concise yet comprehensive books have practical suggestions and exercises which allow personal experience as well as theoretical understanding, and offer a valuable source of information on many important themes.

In the same series

> **the elements of**

zen

david scott & tony doubleday

ELEMENT

Shaftesbury, Dorset · Rockport, Massachusetts · Brisbane, Queensland

Cover design by Max Fairbrother
Illustrations by Uma
Typeset by Falcon Typographic Art Ltd, Edinburgh
Printed and bound in Great Britain by
Biddles Limited, Guildford and King's Lynn

British Library Cataloguing in Publication
data available

Library of Congress Cataloging in Publication
data available

ISBN 1-86204-042-7

CONTENTS

David Scott dedicates this book to Annette Hollins.
Tony Doubleday dedicates this book to his parents.

David Scott and Tony Doubleday would really like to thank
Harry Cook for his contribution to this book. He wrote the
chapter 'Zen and The Martial Arts'. It was presented in such
a clear and explanatory way that it stands just as he wrote it.

We would finally like to thank Genpo Merzel Sensei, Abbot
of Kanzeon Zen Centre. We are both Zen students of his and
continue to be privileged to receive his teachings. Without him
we would not have been able to write this book.

AUTHOR'S NOTE

Tony Doubleday initially began work as a research assistant on this book, but his contribution was so valuable and far ranging that his role soon developed into that of co-writer. However, I accept final responsibility for the authorial editing of this book.

David Scott

Names, Dates and Quotes

Any book on Zen Buddhism runs into trouble about which translations to use for the name of old Zen masters and Zen terminology. There are English translations of original Chinese names (and different systems are in use here) and English translations of the Japanese translations of the Chinese originals as well as straightforward English translations of Japanese names and terms. As you can imagine it can become rather confusing to a non-academic. We have simplified matters by choosing the names and terms that are in most common usage. This means that we have not necessarily been systematic. On the first occasion that a person of historical importance is named we give the date of his birth and death where possible. If this information is not given the person concerned is generally either a contemporary Zen teacher or one who died this century. A sources list is to be found on page 132.

We have used quotes throughout the book but to keep it simple we have not always given chapter and verse notes on the origins of the quote. The further reading list at the back of the book contains the names of all the books used in our research.

INTRODUCTION

We can describe the ingredients and the cooking methods required to make a particular dish but we are unable adequately to convey in words the flavour of the food or the feeling of fullness it can give. The same is true of Zen. One may describe the structure and practicalities of this spiritual tradition but a writer, no matter how talented, cannot give the reader a genuine experience of the essential nature of Zen. For this one must commit oneself to the practice. The potential reader may thus legitimately ask why write a book about Zen. Our answer is twofold:

The original followers of Zen in China and Japan would embark upon their own spiritual journeys by simply choosing a teacher and with faith and trust they would patiently surrender to his wisdom. The approach of the modern Westerner with his or her distinct cultural conditioning is likely to be a more cautious one. Before committing ourselves to a particular path we like to have some intellectual understanding of what it entails and some knowledge of the practical and philosophical values that underpin it. The first aim of *The Elements of Zen* is to provide this information.

Notwithstanding our initial need for a factual understanding of its philosophy, Zen is a non-intellectual tradition and the second reason for writing this book is to provide the reader with just a taste of the very special 'no-mind' flavour of Zen. We cannot get to the core of it by reading but with the help of Zen stories, tales of Zen masters, quotes from Zen texts and a description of Zen teaching methods we can perhaps get some insight into its essence.

Compassion, directness, humour, energy, freedom and absurdity combined together give Zen its own unique flavour. *The Elements of Zen* hopefully embodies a modicum of these qualities.

1 · WHAT IS ZEN?

Enlightenment means seeing through to your own essential nature and this at the same time means seeing through to the essential nature of the cosmos and of all things. For seeing through to essential nature is the window of enlightenment. One may call essential nature truth if one wants to. In Buddhism from ancient times it has been called suchness or Buddha-nature or one Mind. In Zen it has been called nothingness, the one hand, or one's original face. The designations may be different, but the content is completely the same.

Zen master Hakūun Yasutani Roshi (1885–1973)

Zen is a practical method of realizing this Buddha nature. It is a body and mind discipline that requires great effort, perseverance and faith in both the possibility of Enlightenment and in one's own ability to attain it. It is simple, direct and practical and concerned with the here and now. When asked by a monk, 'What is the meaning of Zen?' a Zen master replied 'Have you had your breakfast?' 'Yes', said the monk. 'Then wash your bowl', said the master. Understanding or experiencing one's true or Buddha nature leads to an active acceptance of one's ordinary life and a recognition of its extraordinary quality. Everyday activities are vested with the same importance as worldly ambition. Umon (died 949), a Zen master, when asked how to act in accordance with our true nature replied:

When walking just walk,
When sitting just sit,
Above all, don't wobble.

2

As Umon so clearly demonstrated, the essence of Zen is most directly conveyed in the language of everyday experience and not in the phrases of the theologian or academic.

The pragmatic aim of Zen is to lead the practitioner to a direct experience of life in itself. To eliminate all dualistic distinctions such as I/You, true/false, subject/object and to come to an awareness of life unconditioned by words and concepts.

We obviously need words to communicate ideas but the Zen view is that if we rely only upon them we may be in danger of substituting a knowledge about something for the effort of striving for a direct experience of its reality. The Zen method is to demonstrate Reality, not to describe it in words. Thus Zen training methods are designed, sometimes quite ruthlessly, to give the practitioner a direct experience of unveiled, unadorned Reality.

Ask a Zen teacher, 'What is Zen?' and he is liable to answer with another question: 'Who are you?' or 'What is life?' From his perspective, Zen is first and foremost the experience which the student must recognize in his or her own life. The teacher will recognize that books and lectures can convey a certain amount of useful interpretation and instruction, but he or she will constantly point out their limitations. Information is acquired and passed on from one person to another, unlike the experience of Zen, which is concerned with the nature of our innermost being. In as much as we are content to chase after mere knowledge about Zen, we may become clever academics, but we could fail to confront the mystery of our own existence as human beings, and therefore fail to understand Zen. As the Chinese Zen master, Mumon (1183–1260), warned: 'Endeavouring to interpret clearly, you retard your attainment'.

In seeking for a verbal understanding of Zen we are confronted by the thunderous silence with which the legendary enlightened Buddhist layman, Vimalakirti, answered a question about the nature of Reality. In the Sutra named after him, we are told that Vimalakirti received a visit from a group of the Buddha's senior followers, including the Bodhisattva Manjushri, who was renowned for his wisdom. To test their understandings of the Buddha's teaching, Vimalakirti asked his guests the means by which one aspiring to Enlightenment should come to know Reality as a direct experience. Each of those present spoke in turn, concluding with Manjushri, who said: 'It is my understanding that Reality cannot be grasped by means of words, teaching, debate or speculation. We must go beyond all questions and answers. That is the means to know Reality as a direct experience.' Then Manjushri said to Vimalakirti,

'So, each of us has had our say. Now, you tell us, what is the means by which one aspiring to Enlightenment should come to know Reality as a direct experience?' Vimalakirti kept silent. At that Manjushri exclaimed, 'Excellent, excellent! How can there be true realization of Enlightenment until words and speech are given up?'

Manjushri's answer had been quite correct, but Vimalakirti's answer went far beyond the rights and wrongs of the matter. It was the direct expression of his understanding. To appreciate it we too have to understand the silence of our own hearts.

The word Zen itself is an abbreviation of Zenna or Zenno which is the way the Japanese would read the Chinese characters for Ch'an-na, which in its turn is Chinese for dhyana. This is a Sanskrit word that describes both the act of meditation and the state of non-dualistic consciousness (or other states of consciousness beyond that of ordinary experience) that may arise from its practice.

As one would suspect from the origins of its name, the foundation of Zen practice is za-zen meditation and its specific aim is to lead the practitioner to a full realization of his or her true nature. Zen teaches that the practice of za-zen is the steepest but quickest route to Enlightenment or 'seeing things as they are'. The goal of Zen is Enlightenment and ever-deepening Enlightenment.

To proceed we need then to ask the question, what is Enlightenment? Here again we confront the limitation of information. How are we to understand by words an experience we do not know? If anything, the words just get in the way. They may become concepts or preconceptions that we try to force our experience to fit. For this reason many of the great teachers of Buddhism have assiduously avoided describing Enlightenment in terms around which preconceptions can be formed. Like Manjushri in debate with Vimalakirti they have preferred to describe the experience in predominantly negative terms.

The contribution of Zen teachings has been to leave aside the dialectics of what Enlightenment is or is not, and to present its concrete manifestation in everyday life. Thus the way to practise Zen is not to form some conceptual understanding of what for instance Yasutani Roshi (in the quote opening this chapter) means by essential nature and then go looking for it. Instead it is to become aware of ourselves as we really are and to appreciate what it means to be consciously self-aware. Rarely do we stop to reflect on what it really amounts to when we say 'I think' or

'I feel' or 'I act'; and yet reflection of this sort is the doorway to Enlightenment.

In Japanese, awakening to Enlightenment is called 'Satori' or 'Kensho'. These two terms are often used interchangeably. Although since realization may be sudden or gradual, and more or less profound, it is usual to call limited insight Kensho, and Enlightenment itself Satori or Dai-Kensho (meaning great awakening). A Kensho experience can provisionally be understood in the sense that when discriminative thinking is put aside, there remains an expansive dimension to being, not entirely unknown previously, but which has a significance hitherto ignored. Consequently, the involuntary reaction of anyone for whom Kensho becomes a reality is often one of surprise and amusement; 'Of course! How stupid of me!'

The experience is a little like that of a man who, standing at the automatic cash dispenser outside his bank, struggles to remember the personal identification number of his cash card. For several minutes he is gripped by doubt and frustration whilst, try as he might, he cannot remember it. When eventually it does pop back into his conscious mind it is so familiar to him that he is absolutely certain he has remembered it correctly; and he chuckles to himself that he should have forgotten it in the first place.

The Soto Zen master Kodo Sawaki Roshi said that to practise Zen is to become intimate with the Self. The Self is that expansive dimension to being we have called the Essential Nature. It includes and does not oppose the ego with which we normally identify ourselves, and from which we create the 'persona' we present to others. Zen is not as some believe about destroying or somehow getting rid of the ego, as if it were a physical part of ourselves which could be surgically removed. The ego is the sum total of all our memories, habits, desires, aversions, opinions, thought patterns and so on. It provides our terms of reference for relating in the world and, in that context, is a vital tool. However, it also restricts and frustrates us when we do not see its provisional and limited perspective on life. Fundamentally it is impermanent and insubstantial, and therefore part of a greater emptiness or awareness. In learning intimacy with the Self, ego is transcended, its bondage is escaped, and it can be used freely, compassionately and wisely.

This relationship between ego and Essential Nature was illustrated by the Japanese Zen master Bankei Yotaku (1622–1693) with an analogy from needlework.

The unborn Buddha-mind deals freely and spontaneously with anything that presents itself to it. But if something should happen to make you change the Buddha-mind into thought, then you run into trouble and lose that freedom. Let me give you an example. Suppose a woman is engaged in sewing something. A friend enters the room and begins speaking to her. As long as she both listens to her friend and sews in the Unborn, she has no trouble doing both. But if she gives her attention to her friend's words and a thought arises in her mind as she thinks about what to reply, her hands stop sewing; if she turns her attention to her sewing and thinks about that, she fails to catch everything her friend is saying, and the conversation does not proceed smoothly. In either case, her Buddha-mind has slipped from the place of the Unborn. She has transformed it into thought. As her thoughts fix upon one thing, they're blank to all others, depriving her mind of its freedom.

If the unborn Buddha-mind is the true nature of our ordinary minds then it must follow that it is to be found in the midst of our ordinary lives. In Zen training, intimacy with Self confronts us with the world of everyday forms. This intimacy with the forms of the everyday world then confronts us with the reality of emptiness and impermanence. Eihei Dogen Zenji (1200–1253), the founder of Japanese Soto Zen said:

To learn the way of the Buddha is to learn about oneself. To learn about oneself is to forget oneself. To forget oneself is to be enlightened by everything in the world. To be enlightened by everything is to let fall one's own body and mind.

It is this falling off of one's body and mind that leads to the realization that there is no fixed entity commonly referred to as oneself. There is only boundless, infinite, unobstructed space. In the words of Genpo Sensei, a modern day Zen teacher:

This space, also called 'emptiness' or Shunyata, is no mere vacuity but is real, full and existing. It is the source from which all things arise and return. It cannot be seen, touched, or known, and yet it exists as 'I' and is being freely used by each one of us every moment of the twenty-four hours. It has no shape, no size, no colour, no form, and yet all that we see, hear, feel and touch is 'it'.

It is beyond our intellectual knowing and can never be attained by the rational mind. In other words, it is completely ungraspable. When we suddenly awaken to the clear realization that there is no barrier and never has been, one realizes that one is all things: mountains, rivers, grasses, trees, sun, moon, stars, universe, are all oneself. There is no longer any division or barrier between oneself and others, no longer any feelings of alienation, fear, jealousy or hatred towards others for one knows, and has attested to, the clear fact that there is nothing apart from oneself and therefore nothing to fear. Realizing this naturally results in 'true compassion'. Other people and things are no longer seen as apart from oneself, but, on the contrary, as one's own body.

When we discover our true nature there is a sense in which we have returned home, or rediscovered something of great value. This is a recurring theme in myth and is a point often emphasized in Zen. That is perhaps why we can hear about Vimalakirti's thunderous silence for example and, even without understanding why, feel great affinity for his story.

In conclusion we may say Zen is universal and applicable to anyone anywhere. One of its basic beliefs is that Buddha-nature is inherent in all people and that it is perfect. This true Self has compassion and love of one's fellow creatures, but, as the Buddha said, 'because men's minds have become inverted through delusive thinking they fail to perceive this'. The Zen student aspires to see through the delusion and into his own true Self and thus the nature of all existence. Thus Zen training does not add anything to an individual, on the contrary it shows the path to strip away delusions in order to become what one really is, to come home, in Zen parlance. This coming home involves seeing things more and more truly as they really are.

The philosophy of Zen is finally based on assumptions that cannot be proved by intellectual argument. The only way really to understand Zen is through experiential knowledge. This is gained in the Zen tradition through training methods developed since the time of Bodhidharma, 1500 years ago.

Ideally Zen training involves regular practice of za-zen, membership of a Buddhist community or association (Sangha), direct access to the teachings of a spiritual guide (a roshi) and study of the teachings of the Buddha (the Dharma). The Buddha, the Dharma and the Sangha are known as the Three Treasures.

The characteristics of Zen that set it apart from other Buddhist traditions have been summarized as follows. Firstly, Enlightenment is directly transmitted from master to pupil, outside of orthodox teachings. (In the Zen tradition, the direct transmission of Dharma approval is essential. It has been said that the strength of Zen is this very master-to-disciple, mind-to-mind transmission.) Secondly, there is no dependence on scriptures or other sacred writings. Thirdly, Zen teachers point directly at the human heart. Christmas Humphries (1901–1983), founder of the British Buddhist Society, described Zen as the apotheosis of Buddhism . . . a direct assault upon the citadel of Truth without reliance on concepts of God or soul or salvation.

2 · ORIGINS AND HISTORY OF ZEN

Buddha was born at Kapilavastu;
Enlightened at Magadha;
Taught at Varanasi;
Entered Nirvana at Kusinagara.

Soto Zen mealtime chant

Japanese Zen with its emphasis on the practice of za-zen, koan study and the achievement of satori has its origins in China. Here the first Zen masters taught and the first recognizably Zen monasteries were founded. However, the deepest roots of Zen are in India where Siddhartha Gautama was born, attained Enlightenment and founded the Buddhist religion. His life story is of more than historical interest since for Zen followers he is the supreme model of one who has followed the Way to its end and achieved perfect Enlightenment. The Buddha (a Sanskrit word meaning Awakened One) is no abstract figure of the past but a man with whom a Zen master might feel a personal relationship in his awareness of their shared struggles. The Zen follower believes that each of us has the potential for complete awakening and that the Buddha's path is not reserved for a special few but that it is quite definitely open to all.

The Buddha was born in the sixth century BC in the northwest of India. At his birth his father, Suddhodana, the chief of the Shakya tribe, consulted an astrologer. It was predicted that the young Siddhartha would grow up to be either a world-conquering hero or a great sage.

Suddhodana evidently preferred the first option, and arranged for his son to be brought up in all the kingly and warrior virtues of the day, sheltered so far as possible from anything that might have led his son to question the meaning of life.

Initially, Suddhodana succeeded in his aims, and Siddhartha grew up into a stable and happy young man. He married and his wife bore him a son. However, without any clear perception why, he finally grew restive and found his life unsatisfying. He decided to escape secretly from the confines of the palace and venture out among his father's subjects. For the first time in his life he encountered the realities of sickness, old age and death, and as a result of this experience he became increasingly distressed, and realized that no amount of fatherly protection, comfort or luxury could save him, or anyone else, from the travails of life.

Pondering the problem, and seeking an answer, he decided to become a wandering mendicant. In those times this was the path taken by people seeking to understand mortality and human suffering. So Siddhartha renounced his wealth, power and family and set out in search of the truth. He was about thirty years old, in the prime of life and very determined. He had given up everything for a future that was utterly uncertain. As was the custom, he had no possessions, slept in the open and obtained food by begging.

He travelled from teacher to teacher learning all they knew, but was still unable to resolve his doubt about the meaning of life. In his determination to resolve this problem he subjected himself to all manner of severe austerities, and gained something of a reputation as an ascetic in the process. A small circle of followers gathered around him. Together they fasted, exposed themselves to extremes of heat and cold, and underwent other bodily mortifications. After about five years of this life Siddhartha was close to death from starvation and exhaustion, but still he could not resolve his doubt.

Finally he concluded that the meaning of life was not to be found through extreme asceticism, and he abandoned this practice. We should not overlook the significance of this. In effect he decided that the five or six years during which he had voluntarily subjected himself to the most incredible hardship (and regained some personal status as a result) had been a complete waste of time. Like his initial decision to leave Suddhodana's palace, it must have taken some tremendous self-confidence and courage to acknowledge this. It also testifies to the strength of his personal doubt about the meaning of life, and his faith and determination to resolve it.

For the first time in many years he ate a proper meal. The rest of the group who had by now accepted him as their teacher left in disgust. Profoundly frustrated by his own failure, Siddhartha suddenly remembered a time during his childhood when, seated one day beneath a tree in the palace garden, he spontaneously experienced a state of perfect harmony and peace with life. With renewed determination he now sat down beneath a nearby tree and resolved not to get up again until his doubt about the meaning and purpose of life had been completely satisfied.

Day passed into night, and night gave way to dawn. Then, according to the version of the story followed in Zen, the morning star rose over the horizon. Seeing it, Siddhartha suddenly realized that he had never lacked for the answer to his doubts. Life and death were just passing phenonema on the stage of the Unborn which was nothing other than himself. 'How miraculous!' he exclaimed. 'All living beings are intrinsically enlightened as to the meaning of life and death, they are perfectly endowed with the wisdom and compassion of the Awakened Ones, but because of their delusive thinking they fail to perceive this.' Realizing this truth, his doubt was resolved, and Siddhartha Gautama became Shakyamuni Buddha.

The truth he discovered was so simple, yet subtle, that he doubted anyone would be capable of understanding. However, on reflection, he realized that at least a few people would be ready to respond to his teaching and he set out on a teaching career that was to last nearly forty years, the reverberations of which are felt to this day.

There are as many formulations of the Buddha's teaching (the 'Dharma') as there are schools of Buddhism. The Zen sect claims to transmit the very essence of the Dharma without reliance on the words and letters of its doctrine. This is not to say that Zen ignores canonical Buddhism but rather that, like Vimalakirti, Zen masters consider it more important to manifest the essence of Buddhism than merely to talk about it. So it was that Hui-neng (638–713), the Sixth Patriarch of Chinese Zen, although illiterate and therefore unable to study the Sutras, was able to explain them fully to anyone who cared to read passages to him. Hui-neng once said: 'Do not let yourself be bowled over by the Sutra, you must instead bowl over the Sutra yourself.'

The Buddha's teaching was pragmatic, direct and adapted to the needs of his listeners. He never lost sight of the profound depths of confusion into which most of humanity is plunged, and was ready to use all manner of provisional teachings to help his followers out of their misunderstandings and difficulties. Thus when approached by a woman with her dead baby in her arms seeking solace and some understanding of why such an awful thing had happened to her, he said he could help her, but that first she should bring him a mustard seed from a house that had not known suffering. She went from house to house seeking such a seed, but although many offered seeds, she could not find a house that had not known suffering. So she returned to the Buddha, who said:

> My sister, thou has found,
> Searching for what none finds, that bitter balm
> I had to give thee. He thou lovest slept
> Dead on thy bosom yesterday; today
> Thou knowest the whole world weeps
> With thy woe.

The Buddha developed many tactful methods to lead people to abandon their attachment to the discriminating mind (which he saw as the source of their troubles). He explained why he had to do this in the parable of the burning house:

In a city in a certain country there was a great elder whose house was enormous, but provided with only a single narrow door. This house was terribly dilapidated, and suddenly one day a great fire broke out and began to spread rapidly. Numerous children were inside the house and the elder begged them to come out. They were all engrossed in play, and though it seemed certain they would be burned, they took no notice of the elder, and had no urge to come out.

The elder thought for a moment. He was very strong and might have loaded all the children into some kind of box and carried them out at once. But then he thought that if he did this some might fall out and be burned. So he decided to warn them of the fearsomeness of the fire so that they would come out of their own accord.

In a loud voice he called to them to escape at once, but the children merely glanced up and took no real notice.

The elder then remembered that the children all wanted toy carts, and so he called out to them to come out at once because he had the goat carts, deer carts and bullock carts that they were always wanting.

When the children heard this, they finally paid attention and fell over each other in their push to get out. Thus they escaped from the burning house. The elder was relieved at their safe delivery from harm, and as they began to ask for their carts, he gave to each of them not the ordinary carts they wanted, but carts splendidly decorated with precious things and drawn by great white bullocks.

The symbolism of this story is perhaps fairly obvious. The elder is the Buddha, the burning house is the nature of existence which the Buddha called 'Dukkha' (that is, incapable of giving lasting satisfaction because in every respect it is insubstantial and transitory). The children are humankind, and their play represents the mundane diversions with which we are all so busy that, even though we may be aware vaguely of the life of the true Self, we pay it no need. The goat, deer and bullock carts are the provisional teaching methods, in effect the 'bait' by which the Buddha is able to make us listen and start to practise the Dharma, and the splendid carts pulled by the great white bullocks represent Enlightenment itself, to which the Buddha can only lead us once he has our co-operation and commitment.

The spirit of the entire history of the Buddha's Dharma is perhaps summarized in this story. It has been adapted and expanded upon by all his great Dharma successors. It also demonstrates the provisional nature of what the Buddha taught. He likened his teaching to a raft, useful so long as one is crossing the water, but to be left behind afterwards. This is why in the Zen tradition the Dharma has been called the finger pointing at the moon.

In the Lankavatara Sutra the Buddha is recorded to have said: 'If a man becomes attached to the literal meaning of words . . . in regard to the original state of Enlightenment which is unborn and undying . . . he will come to cherish views either affirmative or negative. As varieties of objects are seen in delusion, and are discriminated as real, statements are erroneously made, discriminations erroneously go on. It is by the ignorant that discriminations go on; it is otherwise by the wise.' And in the Vajraechedika (Diamond) Sutra:

> Thus shall ye think of this fleeting world:
> A star at dawn, a bubble in a stream;
> A flash of lightening in a Summer cloud,
> A flickering lamp, a phantom and a dream.

Although the Dharma has been formulated into the Four Noble Truths, the Eightfold Path, the Five Spiritual Virtues, and Five Hindrances to Practice, the Twelve Links of Conditioned Existence and much more; these are all so many expedient means to bring people to understand the true nature of the human heart and mind. Hence elsewhere in the Sutras we are told that between Enlightenment at Magadha and his death, or paranirvana, at Kusinagara the Buddha uttered not one word of teaching, that the Buddha did not attain Enlightenment beneath the Bodhi-tree at Magadha or at all, and that he eternally sits on the 'Vulture Peak' preaching the Dharma before the assembly (the Sangha).

In *Zen Flesh, Zen Bones* translated by Nyogen Senzaki and Paul Reps, we also find the following:

> Buddha said: 'I consider the positions of kings and rulers as that of dust motes. I observe treasures of golds and gems as so many bricks and pebbles. I look upon the finest silken robes as tattered rags. I see myriad worlds in the universe as small seeds of fruit, and the greatest lake in India as a drop of oil on my foot. I perceive the teachings of the world to be the illusion of magicians. I discern the highest conception of emancipation as a golden brocade in a dream, and view the holy path of the illuminated ones as flowers appearing in one's eyes. I see meditation as a pillar of a mountain, Nirvana as a nightmare of daytime. I look upon judgement of right and wrong as the serpentine dance of a dragon, and the rise and fall of beliefs as but traces left by the four seasons.'

In the Zen tradition it is said that for all his forty years of teaching the Buddha had only one Dharma successor, his senior disciple, Mahakashyapa. This is how D.T. Suzuki tells the story of Mahakashyapa's Dai-kensho:

> The Buddha was one day on the Mount of Vultures, preaching to a congregation of disciples. He did not resort to a long verbal harangue to explain the subject he was treating. He simply raised up before the assembly a bouquet of flowers that one of his disciples had offered to him. Not a word left his mouth. No one understood the meaning of this attitude except the venerable Mahakashyapa who smiled serenely at the master, as if he fully understood the meaning of his silent teaching.
>
> The Buddha, noticing this, solemnly proclaimed: 'I have the most precious spiritual treasure which at this moment I am transmitting to you, O Mahakashyapa.'

In effect the Buddha was saying to Mahakashyapa: 'This flower is the true way and I transmit it to you.' Mahakashyapa had direct insight into the here-and-now experience of 'just these flowers', in the same way that Shakyamuni had experienced 'just the morning star'. The symbols of Enlightenment, the Buddha's robe and bowl, were passed on, and, in the words of the White Lotus Sutra, 'A Buddha together with a Buddha fathomed the reality of all existence'.

Mahakashyapa transmitted the Dharma to Ananda, another of the Buddha's disciples in this way: Ananda asked Kashyapa. 'The world-honoured one gave you the golden robe: did he give you anything else?' (In other words did the Buddha give Mahakashyapa some secret teaching) 'Ananda!' cried Kashyapa. 'Yes Sir!' answered Ananda. 'Knock down the flagpole at the gate!' said Kashyapa. In the shock of hearing and answering, Ananda was totally alive in the moment. There was nothing more for him to grasp.

Katsuki Sekida says of this:

> When a master's lecture was going to take place, a flag was hoisted on the pole at the gate of the temple. But now the pole was to be knocked down. Kashyapa's lecture was over. Knocking down the pole is a dramatic confirmation of the transmission of the Dharma to Ananda. Knocking down the flagpole has another important implication. Knock down your own ego, knock down what you treasure: Enlightenment, Zen, your teacher, the Buddha, everything. This knocking down is used as an independent koan. The teacher will ask: 'How do you knock down the flagpole?'

From Shakyamuni the essence of the Buddha's Enlightenment was transmitted through, in all, twenty-eight generations of Indian Dhyana masters to Bodhidharma in the sixth century AD. Siddhartha Gautama had indeed become a world conquering hero, but not quite in the way his father had planned.

CH'AN (OR ZEN) IN CHINA

In about AD 520 Bodhidharma crossed the Indian Ocean to China. His arrival in the land of the Yellow Emperor marked the beginning of Ch'an and he became the first of the Chinese Patriarchs.

Although various schools of Buddhism were established in China long before Bodhidharma arrived, his reputation as a renowned Dhyana master preceded him and the Chinese Emperor Wu-ti (AD 502–40), a devout Buddhist, called upon Bodhidharma to visit the Imperial Palace to teach. The Emperor had sponsored the construction of a great many Buddhist monasteries and temples, and patronized the teachers of the various Buddhist sects. In accordance with his understanding of their teachings, he assumed that, as a result of all this, he would gain much 'merit' in the form of a happy and prosperous reign, and an auspicious rebirth in what some Buddhist schools called a 'Pure Land': where, unlike on earth, all the conditions of life would be conducive to his attainment of Enlightenment.

The Emperor was delighted to have the opportunity to meet such a profoundly enlightened master, and was eager to know of his spiritual achievements. On meeting Bodhidharma, it is said that the Emperor asked:

'I have built many temples, copied innumerable Sutras and ordained many monks since becoming Emperor. Therefore, I ask you what is my merit?'

'None whatsoever!' answered Bodhidharma.

The Emperor asked: 'Why no merit?'

Bodhidharma replied: 'Doing things for merit has an impure motive and will only bare the puny fruit of rebirth.'

The Emperor, a little put out, then asked: 'What then is the most important principle of Buddhism?'

Bodhidharma replied: 'Vast emptiness. Nothing sacred.'

The Emperor, by now bewildered, and not a little indignant, then asked: 'Who is this that stands before me?'

Bodhidharma replied: 'I don't know.'

When the Emperor did not understand, Bodhidharma crossed the river to Shaolin, where he meditated for nine years facing the wall of a cave.

Wu-ti later discussed the encounter with Bodhidharma with one of his most trusted Buddhist priests. The priest asked: 'Does your Imperial Majesty now know who this person is?' The Emperor said he did not. The Priest said: 'He is the Bodhisattva of compassion, the bearer of the Buddha's heart-seal.' Full of regret, the Emperor wanted to call Bodhidharma back to court, but the priest said: 'Even if you sent for him he would not come. Not even if everyone in China went to petition him.' Nevertheless, Bodhidharma did attract a circle of his own followers and in time confirmed Eka (Chinese Hui K'o) as his own Dharma successor.

Early Dhyana masters quickly found that the Chinese had an indigenous contemplative system of their own in the teachings of Lao-tsu and Ch'ung-tsu (which are collectively called Taoism). The simple way of living in harmony with life associated with Taoism is summed up in the principle 'Wu-wei', meaning 'non-doing' or 'no effort' (in the sense of pursuing illusions of the mind). The classic text of Taoism, the *Tao Te Ching*, begins:

> The Tao that can be told is not the eternal Tao.
> The name that can be named is not the eternal Name.
>
> The unnameable is the eternally real.
> Naming is the origin of all particular things.
>
> Free from desire you realize the mystery
> Caught in desire you see only the manifestations.
>
> Yet mystery and manifestations arise from the same source.
> This source is called darkness.
>
> Darkness within darkness.
> The gateway to all understanding.

The similarities with Dhyana Buddhism were marked, and much of later Ch'an is pervaded by the influence of Taoism, so giving Ch'an its distinctive flavour. Consider, for example the Hsin Hsin Ming, written by the Third Patriarch, Sengstan (Japanese: Sosan) which begins:

> The Great Way is not difficult
> For those who have no preferences.
> When love and hate are both absent
> Everything becomes clear and undistinguished.
> Make the smallest distinction however
> And heaven and earth are set infinitely apart.

After the time of the Fourth Patriarch, Tao-hsin, Ch'an masters began to settle and to found training monasteries, and by the time of the Fifth, Hung-jen (AD 601–74) up to a thousand monks were studying in the same area.

THE SIXTH PATRIARCH

One of the students of Hung-jen's monastery was an illiterate peasant boy who was later to become the Sixth Patriarch. His name was Hui-neng and next to Bodhidharma and Shakyamuni he is perhaps the most revered master in Zen history.

17

In the biographical account of his life, the Platform Sutra of the Sixth Patriarch, he tells how he went to Hung-jen after being filled with illumination on overhearing a monk reading the Diamond Sutra. Hung-jen, recognizing his Enlightenment, set him to work in the kitchen to avoid embarrassing the senior monks. Eight months later, Hung-jen called a meeting of all the monks and announced that if any monk could compose a poem that explained the essence of Zen he would be given the 'transmission' and receive the robe and bowl of office as Sixth Patriarch. The favourite for the title was the head monk, Shen-hsui. He wrote the following verse, unsigned, on a monastery wall in the dead of night:

> Our body is the Bodhi-tree
> And our mind a mirror bright.
> Carefully we clean them hour by hour
> And let no dust alight.

The other monks marvelled at this, and decided it could not be bettered. However, Hui-neng, passing along the corridor asked for the verse to be read out to him (he did not know of Hung-jen's test), and dictated his own poem to go alongside it:

> There is no Bodhi-tree
> Nor stand of a mirror bright.
> Since all is void
> Where can the dust alight?

All were amazed, and the master, recognizing that this was the work of someone who truly understood the essence of mind, erased it lest it put Hui-neng in danger from the wrath of monks jealously loyal to Shen-hsui. Hui-neng was summoned to see the master that same night. He was given the robe and bowl of office (said to be those of Bodhidharma), and was advised to flee south. There followed fifteen years of anonymity before Hui-neng thought the time was right to reveal himself as the Sixth Patriarch. His school of Zen became known as the Southern School, and that of Shen-hsui – which was to die out – as the Northern School.

Such was Hui-neng's genius that he was apparently able to transmit the Dharma to forty-three successors! Thereafter there were many different lines of transmission of Zen, and this was the germ of the development of the two main sects of Zen in Japan today: Soto and Rinzai.

The T'ang Dynasty (AD 620–906) was the Golden Age of Zen in

China. It produced many great masters like Joshu (AD 778–897) and Nansen (AD 748–834), and the stories and anecdotes of these masters were recorded in collections like the Mumonkan, the Hekiganroku, the Shoyoroku and the Tetteki Tosui, and are studied by Zen students to this day. One of the greatest and most influential teachers of this age was Lin-chi.

LIN-CHI (JAPANESE: RINZAI, DIED AD 866)

It is this Ch'an master whose Japanese name is used to denote one of the two major sects of Japanese Zen. Lin-chi was famous for his ruthless and no-nonsense approach to awakening the minds of his students. He was quite capable of striking a questioner to cut through conditioned thought patterns and allow the mind to open up to its true nature. His teaching methods are best illustrated by his own words:

> Followers of the Way, the Buddha-Dharma needs no skilled application. Just be your ordinary selves with nothing further to seek, relieving nature, wearing robes and eating ... If you master the situation you are in, wherever you stand, all becomes true; you can no longer be driven around by circumstances.

> Friends I tell you this: there is no Buddha, no spiritual path to follow, no training and no realization. What are you feverishly running after? Putting a head on top of your own head, you blind idiots! Your head is right where it should be. The trouble lies in your not believing in yourselves enough. Because you don't believe in yourselves you are knocked here and there by all the conditions in which you find yourselves. Being enslaved and turned around by objective situations, you have no freedom whatever, you are not masters of yourselves. Stop turning to the outside and don't be attached to my words either. Just cease clinging to the past and hankering after the future.

ZEN REACHES JAPAN

Prior to its transmission to Japan the two most dominant schools of Ch'an in China were that which traced its lineage from the Sixth Patriarch through Lin-chi, and that which traced its lineage back through Ts'ao-shan Pen-chi (Japanese: Sozan Honjaku, AD 840–901) and Tung-shan Liang-chieh (Japanese: Tozan Ryokai, AD 807–69), which was known as the Ts'ao-tung school in China. In Japan these two schools became known as Rinzai and Soto respectively. Rinzai was first introduced to Japan by the monk Eisai (1141–1215), and Soto by Eihei Dogen Kigen of whom mention has already been made.

In 1184 Eisai built the first Zen temple in Japan. It is called Shofuku-ji and still stands. Later he moved to the Imperial capital, Kyoto, where the Rinzai School became firmly established.

Between the twelfth and fourteenth centuries Rinzai Zen became very popular with the ruling, Samurai class of Japan. The Samurai valued the immediate practicality of the training, which was adapted to suit the urgent needs of those turbulent years. The courage and determination of the warriors made them especially strong Zen students. Rinzai temples opened in Kamakura, the military capital, and an indigenous system of 'Warrior Zen', with its own koan, began to evolve. Meanwhile, Soto Zen developed independently of the political turmoil of the capital.

Dogen was born in 1200. His father died when he was two, and his mother died five years later. At the age of thirteen he went to live with an uncle, a devout Buddhist. The loss of his parents, coupled with his uncle's encouragement, confirmed Dogen's decision to become a monk. Some years later, he joined the monastery of Kenninjo founded by Eisai, and studied with Eisai's Dharma successor, Myozen. During his time at Kenninjo, Dogen completed the training of the Rinzai tradition and received 'Inka', the seal of a master. In spite of this, he had not resolved to his satisfaction the basic dilemma as to the meaning of life. His doubt drove him to undertake the hazardous voyage to China in 1223. There he studied under Master Ju-ching (1163–1228) at T'ien-T'ung monastery. Apparently the training was hard and, at first, Dogen did not have a particularly easy time there. His Dai-Kensho occurred in the following manner:

Following the example of his master, Dogen devoted himself to the practice of zazen day and night. Early one morning, as he was making his usual round of inspection at the beginning of a formal zazen period, Ju-ching discovered one of his monks dozing. Scolding the monk, he said: 'The practice of zazen is the dropping away of body and mind. What do you expect to accomplish by dozing?' Upon hearing these words, Dogen suddenly realized Enlightenment, his mind's eye opening fully. Going to Ju-ching's room to have his Enlightenment confirmed as genuine, Dogen burned some incense and prostrated himself before his master.

'What do you mean by this?' Ju-ching asked.

'I have experienced the dropping away of body and mind,' Dogen replied.

Ju-ching, realizing that Dogen's Enlightenment was genuine, then said: 'You have indeed dropped body and mind!'

Dogen, however, remonstrated: 'I have only just realized Enlightenment, don't sanction me so easily.'

'I'm not sanctioning you easily.'

Dogen, still unsatisfied, persisted: 'What is the basis for your saying that you haven't sanctioned me easily?'

Ju-ching replied: 'Body and mind dropped away!'

Hearing this, Dogen prostrated himself before his master in deep respect and gratitude, showing he had indeed transcended his discriminating mind.

From *Dogen Zen* by Yuho Yokoi.

Dogen returned to Japan in 1227, taking with him copies of certain important Soto Zen texts, nevertheless he said he returned 'empty handed'. The fundamental essence of Zen which he now taught was that practice, or every day activity, is the expression of Enlightenment itself. For this reason he began to place great emphasis on the details of daily activity, and saw each moment as an opportunity to express appreciation of the Buddha-nature. He developed a reputation for hard training and outspoken criticism of other Buddhist sects, including Rinzai.

In 1236 Dogen founded his own temple, and his reputation as a teacher began to grow. Today he is revered as one of Japan's greatest religious geniuses. Dogen would have nothing to do with the military or aristocratic power struggles of his day, and this, combined with his insistence that women and men were all equally capable of accomplishing the Buddha-Way made the Soto tradition truly classless.

It is not within the scope of this book to provide a detailed survey of Dogen's teachings, nevertheless it should be noted that his impact upon Japanese Zen was immeasurable, and no serious student of Zen can afford to disregard his writings.

It is probably not overstating the case to say that after the introduction of Soto and Rinzai to Japan as separate schools they developed and flourished independently of one another for almost 700 years. Whether the vigour of these schools was consistently maintained down the centuries is a matter of some controversy. Hakuin Zenji, for example, is widely regarded in Japan as the seventeenth century reformer of Rinzai Zen, which was by then becoming rather 'stale'. Similarly, the teaching methods of master Bankei broke with the traditional systems altogether.

Over the years each school has criticized the other, and each may be right from its own perspective. Rinzai practitioners have criticized their Soto counterparts for undervaluing the realization of Satori, and the latter have criticized the former for failing to appreciate that the daily practice of the Way is nothing but the actualization of Enlightenment.

It takes someone of the capacity of Dogen himself to obtain the master's approval in one tradition, but then acknowledge that there is still something to be learned from the other. However, that is precisely what Daiun Sogaku Harada Roshi (1872–1963) did. His own Dharma successor, Yasutani Roshi, said of him: 'Although he himself was of the Soto sect, he was unable to find a truly accomplished master of that sect and so went to train at Shogen-ji and then at Nansen-ji, two Rinzai monasteries. At Nansen-ji he eventually grasped the innermost secret of Zen under the guidance of Dokutan Roshi, an outstanding master.' As a result the Dharma successors of Harada Roshi use both Soto and Rinzai teaching methods, and argue that they do so in a way that is innovative, traditional and flexible.

This is mentioned because of the profound influence Yasutani Roshi and others in that lineage have had on the development of Zen in the West.

CONTEMPORARY ZEN IN THE WEST

Although they often associate it with the martial arts, alternative medicine, macrobiotic cooking, motorcycle maintenance and so on, many Westerners have at least heard of Zen today. It has been popularized in films, music, the arts and fiction and there are few large bookshops or libraries which do not carry at least one publication on the subject.

The pioneering work of D.T. Suzuki, Alan Watts and Christmas Humphries, coupled with the scale of cross-cultural communication this century, has also made it very easy for a number of generations of oriental Zen masters to bring the Dharma to the West.

Perhaps because of relationships developed between American occupying forces and Japanese nationals, the first Japanese Zen masters to travel abroad went initially to North America. Early informal gatherings of Westerners led by Nyogen Senzaki and others promoted later interest in formal Zen retreats (sesshin), under the guidance of, for example, Shunryu Suzuki, Hakuin Yasutani and Soen Nakagawa Roshis. By the early seventies formal training centres were well established in America for Soto and Rinzai Zen as well as for Chinese Ch'an and Korean 'Son'.

Like the Japanese monks, Eisai and Dogen, who went to China and returned to Japan with the Dharma, some Westerners interested in Zen spent time in the Far East, and have since returned to found training centres of their own, either as satellites of monasteries in Japan, or independently. These people include Jiyu Kennet Roshi, Venerable Myoko-ni and Philip Kapleau Roshi. Together with the European and American students of Japanese masters in the West who have themselves completed formal training, they represent a generation of indigenous Zen masters, some of whom now have Dharma successors of their own.

Although we are still in the early years of its development, it is becoming clear that Zen in the West is going to be different from its Far Eastern counterparts. This is reflected in students' expectations of themselves, their teachers and the Dharma itself. Thus, as well as remarkable growth, Zen in the West has also witnessed many misunderstandings and difficulties: hard lessons have had to be learned by both students and teachers.

There has been considerable experimentation with the traditional teaching methods, one upshot of which is that teachers have become more willing to talk about and explain Zen than they were in the past. But there are also marked differences of style with the various lineages emerging within the West. Looking at Soto Zen, for example, the Franco-European school founded by Taisen Deshimaru Roshi (1914–82), is very different in its approach to training to Jiyu Kennet Roshi's British and North American Order of Buddhist Contemplatives.

All this is only to be expected as teachers adapt the training to meet the needs of the students. One impression of developed Ch'an is that it became recognizably different from the Indian Mahayana Buddhist Dhyana systems out of which it emerged. Similarly Japanese Soto and Rinzai as they exist today are very different from their twelfth century origins. Since Zen has to do with the appreciation of life, rather than adherence to specific creeds and dogmas, its developed European and North American forms are sure to evolve with recognizably Western cultural characteristics.

It is too soon to say what form those characteristics will eventually take, but at this stage certain concerns and themes seem fairly common in the various Western schools of Zen. Briefly they are:

23

1. Despite Dogen's insistence that men and women are equally capable of accomplishing the Way, there is a marked difference between the modern West and the Far East as to the place and status of women in Zen training. The tendency in the West has been to make no distinction of sex. Training centres, monasteries, sesshin, access to the teachers, have all been made open to everyone. Perhaps as a consequence of this there are far more women pursuing Zen training in the West than in the East.

2. The need for, and distinction between, monastic and lay training has been the subject of much thought and experimentation in the West. Some teachers are very exacting in their demands of those students who wish to become monks, whereas others regard it as a matter of course for anyone who has a regular meditation practice to become a monk if they so wish. The distinction is also blurred because there is no widespread surviving tradition in the West for the laity to support monastic communities. This means that nearly all Western Zen monks must work, at least some of the time, at ordinary jobs to support themselves. As a result, town-based Zen centres, rather than rural monasteries, have been the norm. Where monastic retreat centres have been founded, they tend to house only small residential communities, most people staying for only a few weeks or months at a time.

3. The extent to which Western Zen should adopt the Far Eastern trappings in which Zen is 'packaged' has been treated in widely differing ways. Some Western lineages have made every effort to remove all vestiges of the oriental origins of the practice. Thus all the terms of reference, the Sutras and chants have been translated into near-European equivalents, and forms of presentation have been adopted from the European religious traditions. Others have been much more conservative however, merely, for example, translating certain chants into the vernacular.

The motives for making or refraining from making any changes to the oriental treatment of Zen will be tested in the fullness of time; some will emerge as successful, others will be disregarded as inappropriate. For the time being, the choice of teaching styles and traditions available to the beginner is wide, if not a little bewildering. Perhaps the best and most impartial advice that can be given is that once offered by Dogen Zenji:

> Even people in the secular world must concentrate on one thing
> and learn it thoroughly enough to be able to do it in front of

others rather than learn many things at the same time, without truly accomplishing any of them. This holds all the more true of Buddha-Dharma, which transcends the secular world, and has never been learned or practised from the beginningless beginning. We are still unfamiliar with it. Also, our capacity is poor. If we try to learn many things about this lofty and boundless Buddha-Dharma, we will not attain even one thing. Even if we devote ourselves to only one thing, because of our inferior capacity and nature, it will be difficult to clarify Buddha-Dharma thoroughly in one lifetime. Students, concentrate on one thing.

3 · THE WAY OF ZEN

1. THE JOURNEY TO THE TRUE SELF

There are a number of metaphors for the path of Zen training, the most common being the ten 'Ox-herding' pictures (see Chapter 8); however in the Gakudo-Yojinshu (Guidelines for Studying the Way) Dogen Zenji used another:

> People practising the Way these days have not yet understood what the Way is, so strongly do they desire to gain visible results. Who does not make this mistake? It is like a young man who runs away from his father and his inheritance, and wanders here and there in poverty. Though he is the only child of a wealthy family, he is not aware of this, and endlessly wanders in foreign lands scratching around for work. Indeed all people are like this.

Originally the story of the young man who runs away from home comes from the 'White Lotus' Sutra of Mahayana Buddhism, a text which, as a novice monk, Dogen almost certainly knew by heart.

In the complete story the young man's father, greatly saddened at the loss of his only son, searched for him without success, and eventually settled in a particular town. Being exceedingly wealthy he built himself a fine mansion on a large estate.

Now there came a time when the son felt drawn back towards his own country, and one day he wandered unknowingly into his father's town and approached the mansion looking for work. The young man was really very shabby, and seeing the splendour of the mansion, and the nobility and finery of its owner upon the veranda, decided this was no place for him. So he started to walk on. Meanwhile, his father had never forgotten the young man's face, and immediately recognized him in the crowd outside the mansion. Overjoyed, he sent two of his most important retainers to welcome his son home. Unfortunately, the son, having no idea of these men's intention, and fearing he might be killed or enslaved, fought them off and escaped into the slums. Learning of this, his father decided to send two servants dressed in ragged clothes to seek out his son and offer menial work on the estate.

In this way the young man was lured back into the mansion where he began to work clearing away a huge heap of filth. At night he returned to the slums. As time went by the young man became more comfortable with his surroundings, and accepted an offer of a humble dwelling nearer to the estate. Later, the father dressed himself in work clothes and was able to approach his son and talk with him. The father encouraged the young man in his work, which over time became better quality and more responsible. The son was also told he could visit the mansion house whenever he liked.

Although the son was happy to be treated so well, he retained the conviction that he was subservient to the powerful noble who so kindly employed him; and he felt himself very lowly and unworthy of such generosity. However, he worked faithfully and diligently, and his father continued to give him more and more responsibility until, eventually, he became the manager of the entire estate. After many years the son's sense of inferiority lessened somewhat, and he came to be very friendly with his father. When his death drew near, the father called together all the local dignitaries and his servants and retainers. Before them he announced that the poor man he had taken in and entrusted with the management of his estate was, in fact, his own son to whom all his property now belonged. Only then did the young man realize to his joy that this was his father and such was his inheritance.

As in myth, the story symbolizes the urge of the human psyche towards wholeness. The father, of course, represents Buddha-nature or true Self; he also stands for the Zen teacher. The son is the ego-Self (discriminating mind). The story begins with the predicament in which most people are placed: one of alienation from Buddha-nature which they do not recognize within themselves. In the Gakudo Yojinshu, Dogen Zenji is saying that the degree of people's alienation is represented by the extent to which, like the

27

young man, they have wandered into 'foreign lands', forgotten their 'family' and 'inheritance' and live as 'destitutes', preoccupied with 'scratching a living'. In other words, alienation lies in the extent to which a person's approach to life is based on external gains and successes (what Dogen calls 'visible gain'), as opposed to reflection upon the nature of life-as-it-is. The greater part of humanity is too preoccupied with its habitual needs ('scratching a living') ever to stop and consciously reflect on the way life really is. Indeed the whole direction and 'culture' of society conspires, as it were, against such reflection: thus does humankind live in 'foreign lands'. Nevertheless, there often comes a time when, almost instinctively, even the busiest and outwardly most materialistic person is impelled back towards harmony with his or her life and true Self. In this way the young man was drawn by his own need for work back to his father's gate.

Some people find themselves obliged to reflect upon who they really are when something happens to them which calls into question the meaning of life; when faced for example with the inevitability of death. However, most people are fairly adept at ignoring such issues, or at least marginalizing them as of purely 'religious' interest. Part of the reason for this may be, as the story hints, that the consequence of acknowledging that life is really a mystery to us is very frightening for the ego-Self. The young man ran away in fear from his father's house and his father's high-ranking retainers.

Another aspect is the extent to which, like the son, people regard themselves as unworthy or as failures. Sometimes people want answers to what they regard as 'spiritual' problems, but are afraid to look for them, and doubt their own ability to understand. However, the urge of the Self is towards wholeness, and so in the story the father adopts what in Zen is called compassionate or 'skilful' means. Instead of trying to force his son home, he sends two poorly dressed servants to offer the young man that which he thinks he wants: humble work.

For those in whose lives doubt about the meaning of life does arise it can take on fundamental importance, and is often the reason they turn to Zen, or learn meditation. For others, it often happens that the initial reason they take up Zen is not consciously to do with any need they would call 'spiritual'. More usually people just want some peace of mind, to improve their concentration or to release stress. Perhaps one of their friends happened to mention that meditation might help, so they decide to try.

Zen is not about the extraordinary. Shunryu Suzuki Roshi repeatedly told his American students that it is 'nothing special'. So in the story the young man was set to work in familiar surroundings, clearing up a huge pile of filth. Traditionally clearing the filth is said to symbolize the work of clearing away delusions. The significance of this is important. The pile is enormous. In Mahayana Buddhism and Zen there are four Bodhisattva Vows, the second of which is: 'Desires are inexhaustible, I vow to put an end to them'. Although the son worked faithfully and diligently, the Sutra does not say he got to the end of the pile of filth. His work was itself the Way. Earlier the point was made that Zen practice is not about getting rid of the ego, and it is the same with delusion. There is a famous Mahayana saying: 'The passions are the Bodhi (Enlightenment).' Many people quickly become disillusioned with Zen practice because they take it up imagining that by meditating, for example, they will henceforth experience only peace, love and harmony; whereas what they actually encounter is that pile of filth: all the greed, irritation, jealousy, hatred, feelings of inadequacy and so on that they thought to avoid through Zen. In fact their practice has reached a crucial stage, and the role of the teacher now becomes very important. By training with a teacher the significance of the disillusionment may be understood, and the student is goaded and encouraged to keep going. From the teacher the student will learn that passions are passions to the extent they are indulged or repressed, and Bodhi to the extent they are accepted and allowed to pass through the mind unconditionally and without judgement. (The Zen student does not vow to put an end to desires because in the end he will do so but in order to foster an attitude to training that is indomitable. Zen is simple, but its lessons are tough and have to be learnt time and time again. One Zen master even said his whole life had been a series of mistakes.)

As the young man matured he was given more responsibility, and eventually felt sufficiently self-confident to come and go from the mansion house. He still did not live there, nor yet appreciate who he really was. There is often a feeling in Zen training that one understands more than one is capable of expressing as a living reality. Thus a frequent question asked by people with both a little and a lot of experience of Zen training is: 'How can I make my Zen practice a part of my daily life?' There is the relative calm and serenity of the meditation hall on the one hand, and the mess we live in on the other. This is wandering in and out of the mansion house. Gradually, with maturity and practice, the 'gap' narrows between what has been understood on the one hand, and how we live our lives on the other.

The death of the father, and the son's realization of his real identity represents many things. It is, of course, the end of his journey and the death of the alienation between essential nature and ego-Self. It may be asked whether the son's realization was sudden or gradual. Did he only realize who he was for the first time at the very end? Or is it more likely that he had been slowly coming to suspect it for some time, and at the end his suspicion was merely confirmed as certainty? Are we witnessing here what Christmas Humphries called '. . . A direct assault upon the citadel of Truth', or is it as Suzuki Roshi would have it, that progress is made little by little? He described it thus:

> In a fog, you do not know you are getting wet, but as you keep walking you get wet little by little. If your mind has ideas of progress, you may say: 'Oh, this pace is terrible.' But actually it is not. When you get wet in a fog it is very difficult to dry yourself. So there is no need to worry about progress. It is like studying a foreign language; you cannot do it all of a sudden, but by repeating it over and over again you will master it. This is the Soto way of practice.

The death of the father is also the end of the son's sense of inferiority. Now he sees himself to be this teacher's peer, and recognizes the Buddha within himself. This is the meaning of Mumon's exhortation: 'When you meet the Buddha, you kill him; When you meet the patriarchs, you kill them.' There is also the recognition, master of student, Buddha to Buddha, which in Soto Zen is called 'Shiho', Dharma Transmission, the handing on of the Buddha's teaching. All these things happened when the son was good and ready. Nothing could be forced on him. He had to develop the faith in himself to take on the management of his father's estate. In Zen training the speed of the student's progress will depend on his or her capacity and commitment. Some are quick, others slow. Some want complete realization, others will settle for something less.

Since father and son are elements of the same mind, what, it may be asked, has the son inherited that he did not have originally? In one sense nothing has been gained, but in another the son has come very far indeed. It is a matter of perspective. When asked a similar question by the Emperor of China, Wu-ti, the First Patriarch of Chinese Zen, Bodhidharma, said: 'Vast emptiness, nothing holy.' Pressed further he replied with 'Socratic' certainty that he didn't know. We have already seen that Vimalakirti kept silent.

In the Life of Joshu Jushin we shall encounter some of the answers which this famous Zen master gave to such questions.

2. THE LIFE OF JOSHU JUSHIN (AD 778–897)

The stories that follow centre around the life of Joshu (Chinese Chao-chou Ts'ung-shen), one of the greatest Zen masters of the T'ang Dynasty. They provide wonderful examples of all that is best in Zen. The comments and interpretations offered are no more than that, they are certainly not 'answers' to the problems these stories represent.

When Joshu was still a teenager he began training under his own teacher, Nansen (AD 748–834) the thirty-sixth Patriarch of Zen in succession from Shakyamuni Buddha himself, and whose Zen name derives from the mountain upon which he had sited his monastery. In the koan collection called the Mumonkan there is a record of an early interview between Nansen and Joshu:

> Joshu once asked master Nansen: 'What is the Way?'
> Nansen answered: 'Ordinary mind is the Way.'
> 'Then should we direct ourselves towards it or not?' asked Joshu.
> Nansen said: 'If you try to direct yourself toward it, you go away from it.'
> Joshu then continued: 'If we do not try how can we know it is the way?'
> Nansen replied: 'The Way does not belong to knowing or not knowing. Knowing is delusion. Not knowing is blankness. If you really attain to the Way of No Doubt it is like the great void, so vast and boundless. How can there be a right and wrong in the Way?' At these words Joshu was enlightened.

At this time Joshu was a novice and Nansen was already quite old. Joshu's question is really every beginner's question: What is Zen? On Nansen's answer Genpo Merzel Sensei has said:

> It is translated 'Ordinary mind is the Way', but I have learned to prefer 'natural mind'. 'Ordinary' gives us the implication that it is what we are commonly accustomed to; and with 'Natural' mind – we all know we are not very natural. It is more truthful that the Way is natural mind. It is ordinary mind

31

too, but our common sense understanding of ordinary mind is not very ordinary. It is filled with all kinds of vanities: greed, ambition, jealousy and so forth. When you really get to that ordinary mind it is not what we are commonly accustomed to.

'Mind' here refers to what in Japanese is called 'Shin'. This is not just mind in the sense of the brain, but it is the heart-mind or spirit. One could also say the natural heart is the Way. Joshu asked whether he should search for the ordinary mind. Nansen said by searching he would stray from it. The trouble is, as Joshu's persistent questioning of Nansen demonstrates, it is not enough for the beginner simply to be told this. If one's life is a mess it is very hard to accept that one is the Buddha already. Joshu was looking for a way to become Buddha, and on the face of it, his persistence was quite legitimate. However, his idea of what Enlightenment was, was the very thing that was keeping him from realizing it. From the absolute point of view Joshu was already enlightened, from the relative point of view he didn't see it.

Nansen said that the Way does not belong to knowing or not knowing. In other words it just is. Knowing is illusion, not knowing is blankness, ignorance. When there is no doubt about this, there is just the unborn Buddha-mind. So seeing, Joshu had Kensho.

Mumon, the compiler of the Mumonkan, said of this story: 'Questioned by Joshu, Nansen immediately shows that the tile is disintegrating, the ice is melting, no communication whatsoever is possible.' Joshu's attachment to his ideas and preconceptions dropped away, and he had a glimpse of the nature of the Unborn. Of this, he said of himself: 'I was ruined and homeless'. Mumon continued: 'I doubt though if Joshu reached the point that Nansen did. He needed thirty more years of study.' Mumon wrote a poem on this story:

> Hundreds of flowers in the spring;
> The moon in the autumn;
> A cool breeze in the summer,
> and snow in the winter.
> If there is no vain cloud in your mind
> for you it is a good season.

Later, when Joshu was away, the monks of the eastern and western halls of Nansen's monastery began to quarrel. There was evidently some rivalry between them, and for the purposes of this story it had crystallized around a cat. Seeing the monks arguing over possession of a cat Nansen held it up and said to them:

> If you can say a word of Zen you will save the cat. If not, I will cut it in two. No one could speak, and Nansen killed the cat. That evening, when Joshu returned, Nansen told him what had happened. Joshu took off his sandal, placed it on his head, and walked out. 'If you had been there, you would have saved the cat,' Nansen remarked.

In the previous story Joshu learned that when there is attachment to notions of Enlightenment and delusion, knowing and not knowing, one is already wandering from the Way. This story illustrates the same principle, but this time, unlike the monks of the eastern and western halls, Joshu is not trapped.

Behind all the argument there is attachment to right and wrong, good and bad, mine and yours and so on. By his action Nansen was asking the monks how such disputes are to be settled.

Dogen Zenji said of this story: 'If I were Nansen I should say: "If you answer, I will kill it; if you don't answer, I will kill it."' The modern Zen teacher, Katsuki Sekida has said: 'If I were the monks I should say, "We cannot answer; please cut the cat in two", or I should say, "The master knows how to cut it into two pieces, but he does not know how to cut it into one piece."' Dogen also said: 'If I were Nansen and the monks could find no answer, I should say, "You could not answer" and put down the cat.' Joshu's answer was to place his sandal on his head and walk out. It is important to understand that there was no artifice in this, as there would be if when asked the same question in our own training we merely copied Joshu. He acted spontaneously and intuitively. By such an answer Mumon says:

> When the sword is snatched away, even Nansen begs for his life.

It is worth reflecting on an aspect of this story which sometimes concerns newcomers. Did Nansen literally kill the cat? If so, how could he do it if Zen is supposed to be about compassion? This is the beauty of the koan. Straightaway it entraps the reader in considerations of good and bad, right and wrong, and above all the shoulds and should nots of a so-called holy life. How can one tell the truth but still be compassionate? Truth can hurt. By taking a cat for its theme the koan confronts the reader with his or her own sentimentality. No one could choose to kill a harmless kitten and then claim to be compassionate. However by killing the cat Nansen is displaying how the vanities to which we cling are as dear to us as a little kitten. He is saying that to experience Daikensho one must be ready to give up everything.

'Killing the cat' poses a problem about truth and compassion which every Zen student may have to face at least once in life. Zen is first and last about awakening to Enlightenment. In that context this story overflows with Nansen's compassion. It is only when used to rationalize ulterior motives that it can be debased. (For an interesting example of such debasement see Yukio Mishima's novel *The Temple of the Golden Pavilion* in which the character Kagiwara gives a particularly pernicious interpretation of this koan.)

Joshu trained with his teacher for almost forty years. He was about fifty-six years old when Nansen died. If he followed the Chinese custom of remaining at the monastery tending the dead master's grave for a few years, he was almost sixty before he left Mount Nansen. It is difficult to contemplate the maturity of Joshu's awakening after so long a time with his teacher. He was very young when he understood 'Ordinary mind is the way'. How much of the old egocentric Joshu remained? Many years later Joshu was asked what he had learned from Nansen:

A monk asked Joshu: 'I have heard that you closely followed Nansen. Is that true?' Joshu said: 'Chinshou produces a big radish.'

Katsuki Sekida says:

This was an unpleasant question. The monk had an axe to grind. A clumsy answer might well have lead to some kind of trouble. . . . Chinshou was a district near the town of Joshu famous for producing big, fine radishes. What did Joshu mean by his answer? Had he been an Englishman, he might have said: 'England has produced Shakespeare'; or as an American: 'America has produced Lincoln'. In plain words Joshu was saying: 'Like father, like son,' but he gave the man nothing to take advantage of.

Even after forty years with Nansen, Joshu did not begin to teach right away. First he went on pilgrimage looking for other masters against whom to test his understanding. In those days not all the great masters of the Way lived in monasteries. Some were mountain hermits.

> Joshu went to a hermit's cottage and asked: 'Is the master in? Is the master in?' The hermit raised his fist. Joshu said: 'The water is too shallow to anchor here,' and he went away. Coming to another hermit's cottage, he asked again: 'Is the master in? Is the master in?' This hermit too raised his fist. Joshu said: 'Free to give, free to take, free to kill, free to save,' and he made a deep bow.

Mumon asks about this. 'Both raised their fists; why was one accepted and the other rejected? Tell me what is the difficulty here?' Mumon says that if one is able to resolve this problem one will realize that: 'Joshu's tongue has no bone in it, now helping others up, now knocking them down, with perfect freedom.' (In other words he fully comprehended the essence of Zen.) 'However,' Mumon continues, 'the two hermits could also see through Joshu. If you say there is anything to choose between the two hermits you have no eye of realization. If you say there is no choice between the two you have no eye of realization.'

There are many reasons to raise a fist against another. For example the following may be an analogy for Joshu's first encounter. There was once a group of British Buddhists who went to visit an English coastal town on private business. Whilst there, they decided to make an unannounced call on a local meditation centre. Unable to elicit any reponse by ringing the front door bell they were about to leave when, looking through a window light in the footway, one of them noticed the feet of a resident at the centre walk across the carpet of the basement room. So he knocked on the basement window to attract attention. Whereupon the person inside was heard to shout: 'Get lost! I'm trying to meditate.' The group moved on.

However, by asking, 'Is the master in?' Joshu was asking about the mind in the sense of essential nature: 'Is the Buddha-mind at home?' The hermits must have thought this an absurd question by any standard. No wonder they raised their fists. It is part of the beauty of Joshu's understanding that he could ask such questions and receive the consequences so freely. To the group outside the meditation centre the hostility from within was hilariously funny, but also rather offensive.

After twenty years of wandering Joshu founded a training monastery in the town of Ch'ao Ch'ou after which he is known to posterity. He was about eighty-four years old.

As the Dharma successor to the great Nansen his fame spread quickly and he drew monks to him. It is as a teacher that Joshu is best remembered. Although loyal to Nansen he developed a subtle style all his own.

Leonardo da Vinci once said: 'The true disciple surpasses the master.' This can certainly be said of Joshu. As quoted already in the first chapter but worth repeating here:

> A monk once came to Joshu at breakfast time and said: 'I have just entered this monastery. Please teach me.'
> 'Have you eaten your rice porridge yet?' asked Joshu.
> 'Yes, I have,' replied the monk.
> 'Then you had better wash your bowl,' said Joshu.

Joshu was telling the monk that the flavour of Zen and the flavour of rice porridge are one and the same. It is not that there is anything special about rice porridge; merely that there is nothing special about Zen. The Way of Zen is the way of ordinary life. However, from the standpoint of the monk (and indeed Joshu as a young man), this is hard to accept. It is all too tempting to look for a hidden, esoteric meaning. Yet Joshu was hiding nothing from the monk. Mumon said: 'When he opens his mouth, Joshu shows his gallbladder. He displays his heart and liver.' As before, in Joshu's own case, Mumon was suspicious of the understanding of the monk: 'I wonder whether this monk really did hear the truth. I hope he did not mistake the bell for a jar.' The bell used in a Zen meditation hall is shaped like a jar or a bowl and could conceivably be confused for either. Mumon wondered whether the monk had really seen the truth for what it is.

Although the monk had just entered Joshu's monastery he was not necessarily a beginner in Zen. He could have been someone who had trained for years, in Zen or some other tradition, but had yet to see the Buddha-mind as his everyday life. One can imagine how dissatisfied and disillusioned he might have felt about this, particularly if he thought he had given everything up to find the truth. No doubt his request for the teaching was in absolute earnest, otherwise he would not have dared to be so direct as to interrupt the monastic routine at breakfast time. However, behind his request there was an assumption that there was some special understanding which he lacked.

Joshu's reply went to the root of his difficulty, and confronted him with the question: What are you expecting? But Joshu did this very skilfully, pointing the monk right back at the monastic routine, the monk's ordinary daily life.

Evidently the monk did not immediately see what Joshu was

driving at. Like most of us he could not abandon his preconceptions that easily, and it is this which Mumon recognized. Moreover, in front of the Zen master the monk probably felt nervous and ill at ease, whilst at the same time wanting to make a good impression. In such a situation people often start to feel slow and dull-witted. This makes them fall back on familiar behavioural response patterns, and for the teacher it is a helpful measure of the student's real understanding. The monk's reply – 'Yes, I have.' – is straightforward; but it does not suggest he saw any connection between Joshu's question and his own request for the teaching. So Joshu made his point again: 'Then you had better wash your bowl.' Perhaps the monk was still expecting more, looking for the hidden meaning – mistaking the bell for the jar. Of this koan Mumon asked:

Don't you know that flame is fire?
Your rice has been long cooked.

Very likely the monk had to put his hand into the fire many times; in Zen training one makes the same mistakes over and over. Mumon knew this, but nevertheless throws open a challenge: the attainment of Enlightenment and ordinary life are one, but who is ready to taste it?

Another of Joshu's monks asked him:

What is the meaning of Bodhidharma's coming to China? (This was a common question in those times. It means: What is the essence of Zen?).
Joshu said: The oak tree in the garden.

We have already seen how Vimalakirti and Bodhidharma answered much the same question. The beauty of Joshu's answer is that it is so natural. Apart from life as-it-is, Joshu had nothing to offer this monk. In that moment the essence of Zen was just the oak tree standing in the monastery garden. No doubt there were many fine trees in the monastery grounds, and Joshu may have often sat contemplating their splendour, appreciating every branch and bough, but that is not the point here. Joshu said that the essence of Buddhism is the oak tree in the garden for the same reason Zen master Ummon said the Buddha is a piece of 'dried dung': because it's true. Dogen Zenji pointed out:

Even if up to now, you have thought that a Buddha has excellent characteristics like Shakyamuni or Amitabha, radiates a halo, has the virtue of preaching the Dharma and benefiting living beings, you should believe your teacher if he says the Buddha is nothing but a toad or an earthworm. Throw away your former ideas. However, if you look for some excellent characteristics, a halo, or other virtues of a Buddha on a toad or earthworm, you will still not have reformed your discriminating mind. Just understand that what you see right now is Buddha.

Mumon has already cautioned against mistaking the bell for a jar: the core of the problem is the fundamental distinction we all tend to make between the 'spiritual' on the one hand, and the 'mundane' on the other. There is a very seductive and romantic image attached to so-called spiritual paths. The notion of 'cosmic' or 'super' consciousness is exciting: it promises escape from what can otherwise seem a sad and humdrum life. Unfortunately, so long as we think in this way, our *idea* of higher consciousness will remain no more than that. It is only by fearlessly confronting life as it is, in all its monotony, misery or whatever that one can come to understand, in the words of Yasutani Roshi, that: 'Existence is an inseparable whole, each one of us embracing the cosmos in its totality'.

To someone determined to escape the travail of the ordinary this message is a bit deflating; however, it is to them that Joshu was talking. Unfortunately, as Dogen Zenji said in the thirteenth century:

Students today however still cling to their own discriminating minds. Their thinking is based on their own personal views that the Buddha must be 'such and such'. If . . . [what the teacher tells them] . . . goes against their ideas they say the Buddha cannot be that way. Having such an attitude, wandering here and there in delusion, searching for what conforms to their own preconceptions, few of them ever make any progress whatsoever in the Buddha Way.

Modern Zen masters will tell you it is no different today!

Hopefully the reader is by now getting some impression of the importance of the teacher in Zen training. Few people will push themselves further than it feels comfortable to go, and it is only by training under a teacher that they are compelled to make the leap beyond discriminating mind, and indeed become truly accomplished followers of the Zen way. Genpo Merzel Sensei lived completely alone and practised meditation for a year before he began training under his own teacher, Taizan Maezumi Roshi. He has said that, for him, one of the hardest things to come to terms with was how Maezumi Roshi actually was: 'I had some ideas about how an enlightened master should behave ... and, I don't know why, but he just refused to conform to them. In fact, it seemed like he purposely refused!' Our expectations of the teacher will reflect our own expectations of Enlightenment.

A monk said to Joshu: 'The stone bridge of Joshu is widely renowned, but coming here I see only a set of stepping stones.'

(Although famous throughout China, the stone bridge at the town of Ch'ao Ch'ou was only a series of stepping stones. However, what the monk was implying was: 'Zen master Joshu is renowned, but coming here to see him I see only an insignificant-looking monk.')

Joshu replied: 'You see only the stepping stones. You do not see the stone bridge.' 'What is the stone bridge?' asked the monk. 'It lets donkeys cross over and horses cross over,' said Joshu.

Apparently Joshu did not look the part and the monk was not impressed. He wanted to know who the old man was, and what he had to teach. Seemingly Joshu made no attempt to display any measure of understanding (of Zen); his answer is almost matter of fact. It shows the ease with which he could bring high expectations back down to earth.

On another occasion a monk entered Joshu's room for 'Sanzen' (a private interview), and found him sitting with his head covered by a robe. Taken aback, the monk retreated from the room.

Perhaps the monk expected the teacher to be sitting there with a straight back, alert and full of energy, eyes sharply focused on the door, ready to pierce the monk through with a glance. Instead Joshu looked half asleep, and was possibly even shivering as he huddled under his cowl. Seeing that bent old body crouching before him, very likely the monk thought it better not to disturb him, poor old boy.

'Brother!' said Joshu, 'Do not say I did not receive your sanzen.'

The Zen teacher, Nyogen Senzaki (1876–1958), said of this encounter:

It was probably a cold evening, and Chao-chou covered his head with his robe, heavy with mending and stitching. Since the monk had no right to enter the teacher's room for anything but Zen, why did he hesitate and retreat? Fugai said: 'The monk was a stupid fellow, thinking the master slept like any other absent-minded person. But even a sleeping tiger has a strong vibration around it. The monk was like a person passing through a diamond mine with empty hands. See the brilliance of Chao-chou's loving kindness when he says: "Brother, do not say I did not receive your sanzen." The monk should have bowed and received Dharma at that moment. It is a pity he was deaf and blind.'

The primary function of the teacher is to bring the student to realization. Perhaps the most famous example of this from the whole of the Golden Age of Chinese Zen is contained in this last story from the life of Joshu.

A monk asked Joshu: 'Does a dog have the Buddha-nature?' Joshu answered: 'Mu!'

Of the many hundreds of koan derived from Chinese and Japanese sources, maybe only Hakuin's 'Sound of one hand clapping' is better known than this. Mumon called Joshu's Mu the 'Gateless Gate' of Zen: 'If you pass through it, you will not only see Joshu face to face, but you will go hand in hand with the successive patriarchs, entangling your eyebrows with theirs, seeing with the same eyes, hearing with the same ears. Isn't that a delightful prospect? Wouldn't you like to pass this barrier?'

Generations of Zen trainees have been set to work on Joshu's Mu. Usually it is the first koan a student is given, and its resolution to the satisfaction of the teacher has a fundamental effect on the student's attitude to life thereafter. So what is this koan all about? Katsuki Sekida has outlined four sets of circumstances in which any straightforward question about Zen may be asked:

1. A beginner seriously asks what is the fundamental principle of Buddhism.
2. A student has achieved advanced understanding and demonstrates it by a question of his teacher.
3. 'Dharma combat': where one Zen practitioner questions another to test his or her understanding.
4. As a means of intimate exchange between teacher and senior student.

For the purposes of this book, we have generally taken the perspective of the beginner with a serious question about fundamental principles. In the case of Joshu's Mu, it is useful to imagine the monk as oneself. In the Atvatamsaka Sutra we have read that, on attaining Enlightenment, the Buddha said: 'All living things are Buddhas, endowed with wisdom and virtue . . .' By asking whether a dog has Buddha-nature the monk was not seeking merely to satisfy his curiosity on a particular point of doctrine, his question was really: If, as you say, and as the Sutras say, all beings have the Buddha-nature why can't I see it? His doubt was much the same as that of anyone hearing about Buddha-nature for the first time. It is worth asking oneself how Joshu might have helped him. For example, would the monk have been any the wiser if Joshu had said 'Yes'? Joshu was not concerned merely to agree or disagree with a theory. He wanted the monk to see the truth for himself.

'Mu' is actually the Japanese rendition of Joshu's reply. In the Chinese his humour comes across more clearly: 'Wu!' Did he speak or bark? One can perhaps imagine the effect on the monk! 'Wu' means 'No' or 'Not', but Joshu was asking the monk where Buddha-nature is to be found in a dog, if not in the very perfection of its dogginess! The thing the monk was searching for, and could not find, was his own preconception of Buddha-nature. He could not find it because there is nothing capable of corresponding to it. The beauty of Joshu's answer is that he was able to illustrate the Buddha-nature of a dog and cut through the monk's delusive thinking in that one word. Mumon said:

> The dog, the Buddha-nature,
> The pronouncement, perfect and final.
> Before you say it has or has not,
> You are a dead man on the spot.

According to tradition, Joshu continued to teach until his death at the age of 119. Nyogen Senzaki said of him: 'His Zen was as ripe and mellow as old wine . . . He used neither the "big stick" nor the harsh voice of other masters, but the few words he spoke brimmed with Zen.'

4 · ZEN PRACTICE

The rewards of study lie therein.

Confucius

Realization lies in the practice.

The Buddha

I have never heard of anyone who has earned rewards without studying or who attained realization without practice.

Dogen Zenji

INTRODUCTION

The basic training methods of most schools of Zen, whether Soto or Rinzai, are similar although each of them will differ in the emphasis they put on different practices and in the detail of particular techniques, postures, rituals and so on. The information given in this chapter is of a general nature and if you start training with a Zen group or already belong to one you may find that they have different practice methods from those outlined here. This would be quite usual.

Very simply, the Rinzai schools of Zen place emphasis on koan study as a practice *towards* Enlightenment while the Soto schools concentrate on practice *as* Enlightenment and may not use any koan work in their practice. There are some schools that make use of the teaching methods of both the Soto and Rinzai traditions and the teacher may choose to ask a student to emphasize a particular practice depending on what is individually appropriate to them. However, in all schools of Zen the real core of the practice is za-zen (or seated meditation) and we begin this chapter with an introduction to za-zen.

ZA-ZEN

A place to sit

If you are able, choose somewhere that is quiet and where you will not be disturbed. Keep the area thoroughly clean and, if you can, use the same place every time you do za-zen. Ideally the area you use should be just for your za-zen practice. You may wish to install a small altar on which to place a statue of the Buddha or other inspirational figure, an incense holder and perhaps a tiny vase for flowers, although none of these things is in any way essential. The temperature should be comfortable, that is warm in the winter and cool in the summer. The lighting should be normal, neither too dark nor too light. Natural lighting, when available, is the best. The essential idea is to maintain continuity so that whenever you enter the area set aside for za-zen the setting and the smell (if you use incense) are the same. In this way you will begin to associate za-zen practice with these surroundings and you will be able to settle down more quickly.

Times of Practice

It is best to practise za-zen at a regular time or times every day. Early morning, noon, early evening and before going to bed are the best times. If you can only find time for one session, a morning sitting is the one to aim for. If you wish to sit twice a day, the morning and before bedtime sittings are the best. To begin with, fifteen to twenty minutes is enough. Build up to thirty minutes to an hour, depending on your particular situation. Posture is discussed below but to start with you can use a chair or stool, or halfway through a period of 'sitting' change to a chair or stool to give aching knees, ankles and so on a rest. Remember, however, that the quickest way to get a posture you can hold for a reasonable length of time is to stay in it through the discomfort. But, having said that, initially exercise in moderation.

Posture

There are a number of postures that can be used and you should try each of them to discover which suits you best. This does not mean that you should not persevere with one of the more stable postures just because it seems, at first testing, uncomfortable. Patience and practice are needed to get good posture.

The recommended postures are described here in increasing order of their stability, balance and conduciveness to good practice. It is perfectly acceptable to start with position 1; very few people can sit in position 5 to begin with. In all postures the ideal is to sit so that the body is perfectly upright and a vertical line can be drawn from the centre of your forehead, nose, chin, throat and navel. This is achieved by pushing the waist forward and the abdomen out. In this position the weight of the body is focused on the belly or lower abdomen. This area is the focus of za-zen breathing and concentration. Eyes are half-open and softly focused on the ground about 3 to 6 feet (1 to 2 metres) in front of you. In some schools of Zen it is also allowable to keep the eyes closed (as long as you do not doze off!). Generally, in Soto Zen, it is recommended to sit facing a blank wall so that there are no visual distractions.

Position 1

This is for people who are very stiff through lack of exercise or because of age. Sit on a stool or chair that is of a height that allows you to set your feet firmly on the ground. If you are tall, adjust your height with a firm cushion on the seat or, if small, a thick plank of wood on the floor beneath your feet. Set your back straight, shoulders down, and hold the head upright, as though a thin line of cotton runs from your head to the ceiling, stretching out the vertebrae of the spine into a natural alignment. Rest your hands on your lap, right hand under left hand, palms turned upwards. The thumbs touch at the tips and form a parallel line with your fingers. (See mudra illustration page 46.)

For the next four positions you need a folded blanket about 3 feet (1 metre) square and a firm cushion. Set the cushion on the

Chair Position (Position 1)

blanket; the postures are taken up with the cushion under your bottom.

Position 2
This is the easiest position for beginners. Straddle the mat so that you are sitting on your knees, shins and insteps and bottom. A triangle is formed by your knees and bottom. Head, shoulders and hands are the same as in position 1.

Position 3
This is the Burmese position, a posture popular with Western followers of Zen. The legs are crossed but both feet are flat on

45

Mudra

Seiza (Position 2)

46

Burmese Position (Position 3)

the blanket. The bottom is situated on the first third to a half of the cushion. Both knees should be touching the blanket. If they are not you may help them down by putting a second cushion under your bottom or you can place a small cushion under the knee or knees that stick up. It is important to be sitting on a firm base, formed by the triangle of your knees and bottom. Head, shoulders and hands are the same as in position 1, otherwise it is very difficult to keep the back straight and relax the breathing into the posture.

Position 4

This is the half-lotus position. The left foot is under the right thigh and the right foot is on the left thigh or vice versa. Both

Half-Lotus Position (Position 4)

variations are equally as good. This position is quite difficult for the beginner but supports the lower back better than positions 2 and 3. If you adopt this posture it is important to use alternate leg positions each time, otherwise you will find that you tend to lean to one side.

Position 5

This is the full lotus position in which the right foot rests on the left thigh and the left foot rests on the right thigh. The lotus is the best sitting position since it forms a perfect triangle between the knees and bottom strongly supporting the lower back; and produces great

48

Full-Lotus Position (Position 5)

stability. Unfortunately, the lotus is also the most difficult to achieve and usually out of reach of the beginner and even many mature students. Do not worry if you cannot 'do a lotus' – most of us are in the same position.

Clothes and Equipment

Loose clothing is essential to allow you to sit and breathe freely. Dark clothing, black preferably, is recommended, particularly if you sit with a Zen group. Bright colours may distract the concentration of others. Whatever clothes you wear they should be clean and fresh.

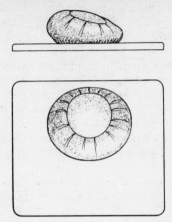

Zafu and Zabuton (Sitting Mat and Cushion)

You will need a firm cushion which should be placed on a flat blanket if the floor is hard or, if not, directly onto the carpet. In Zen monasteries and Zen sitting groups monks and lay people usually sit on a small, black, round cushion called a zafu which is placed on a black mat called a zabuton (about 3 feet/1 metre square). Zafus are approximately 15 inches/38 centimetres in diameter and between 2 and 4 inches/5–10 centimetres thick. They are normally packed tight with kapok. Some people use two zafu or make one higher by placing another cushion or a folded blanket underneath it.

Counting Breaths

After getting into a good posture our first practice to help focus attention is to start counting breaths. To begin with in your practice you can count the in-breaths and the out-breaths. Thus as you inhale count one and as you exhale count two. The count should be inaudible. Do not try to control the breath. Let it follow its own rhythm. As you are counting you will inevitably have some thought or other. If you become distracted by it, you will not always immediately realize you have been caught up. As soon as you notice you have stopped counting breaths begin again at one . . . If you can reach ten without an interfering thought, go back to one and start again. Do the same if you find you have counted beyond ten. Do not be surprised if it takes a lot of practice before you can control your mind to concentrate only on your breaths. Incidentally, be sure not to force your breath. Just watch it and count the breaths as they come. After some practice you could start counting only the out-breaths (or the in-breaths).

For most of us many weeks or months will pass by before we can truly reach the count of ten without a distracting thought. This is quite natural since what we are doing is developing our ability just to be completely present in the moment. Gradually we do learn just to sit for longer and longer periods but for most of us the feeling of having nothing to do is most uncomfortable and our minds will try to fill the gap with an amazing variety of thoughts (see below).

Do not see this practice of counting breaths as something that is easy and one which you wish to move quickly on from. Sitting in za-zen and counting breaths is a complete practice and one which deserves our full attention if we are not to waste our time on the cushion.

Thoughts Arising in Za-zen

Whenever we practise za-zen we will find thoughts arising. This is normal and unavoidable. The technique to deal with them is just to observe them, let them pass and then return to your breathing. Do not be tempted to get hooked into them or you will go off on a long train of thought and you may just as well have given your time to something other than za-zen. Equally do not try to suppress your thoughts, which is almost impossible anyway. Watch them without judgement and allow them to pass like clouds in the sky. We should also try to avoid having intentional thoughts and images. We need to let go of all our stuff about the meaning of life, work, family, politics, the sexy man or woman on the cushion opposite, how good or bad the Roshi or instructor is, how much our knees are hurting or whatever and just be there sitting in za-zen and counting breaths.

Master Dogen said in his treatise *Shobogenzo*, 'Za-zen by a beginner is also the whole experience of the fundamental truth.' Another Zen teacher said, 'When we do za-zen we sit immediately in the same condition of body and mind as Gautama Buddha, and in this sense there is no difference between men of experience and beginners in this condition.' And Dogen once again, '. . . there is no question here at all of being intelligent or stupid, nor is there any difference between the quick-witted and the dull. If you exert yourself singlemindedly (in

51

za-zen), this is practising the Way itself. Practice and realization leave not a trace of impurity, and the person who advances in the Way is an ordinary person.'

Za-zen Checklist

The following is a za-zen checklist from a booklet *Beginning Zen* by David Kenshu Brandon.

1. Sit on the forward half of your zafu (black round cushion).
2. Arrange your legs – full lotus, half lotus, Burmese, kneeling or chair; choose the position you can sustain most comfortably and with stability.
3. Centre your spine by swaying in decreasing arcs.
4. Straighten and extend your spine and align your head (by 'pushing up ceiling' and then relaxing). Origin of thrust is at small of back. Belly and buttocks both protrude slightly.
5. **Head** – shouldn't tilt forward or lean to either side.
   Ears – should be parallel with shoulders.
   Tip of nose – centred over navel.
   Chin – tucked in slightly.
6. **Eyes** – neither fully opened nor fully closed, lowered to 45 degree angle; unfocused, 'gazing' at direction of floor 3 to 4 feet in front. If you are closer than that to a wall, then 'look through it', at where the floor would be. Thus, blinking is minimized.
7. **Mouth** – lips and teeth closed; place the tip of the tongue against the roof of the mouth, just behind the front teeth. Swallow any saliva in your mouth, and evacuate the air so there is a slight vacuum. This inhibits salivation.
8. **Hands** – 'cosmic' mudra:
   right – palm up, 'blade' against lower belly.
   left – atop right, middle knuckles overlap.
   thumb – tips lightly touch, forming an oval.
9. Make sure your whole body is arranged the way you want it before beginning za-zen.
10. Keep as still as possible during za-zen.

After Counting Breaths

After a few months of counting breaths you may wish to move onto other Zen training methods. These may range from different

Kinhin

breathing techniques to koan study or shinkantaza (see below) but at this stage it would be best to find a teacher or Zen group to join.

Contact addresses are in the back of the book together with a guide to further reading.

Kinhin

In a formal session of za-zen the time is usually divided into equal periods of za-zen which are anything between 20 and 50 minutes long interspersed by periods of kinhin (of 5 minutes or slightly longer). Kinhin allows you movement to shake off sleepiness and a break from the za-zen position (a chance to cure numbness in the legs) while allowing you to maintain good posture, even breathing and focused awareness. If za-zen is viewed as the way the Buddha sits then kinhin may be seen as the way the Buddha walks.

The hands' position for kinhin is as follows. Put the thumb of the

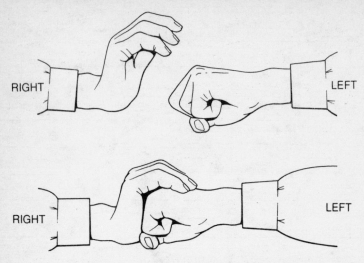

PALMS SHOULD BE FACING TOWARDS BODY

Hand Positions for Kinhin

left hand in the middle of the palm and make a fist around it. Turn this hand to face your chest or, in some schools, downwards in front of your chest. Cover your left hand with the palm of your right hand (see diagram above). Keep your elbows away from your body so that you make a straight line with your arms. If your elbows come to rest gently on your body that is acceptable. Now straighten the posture of your body, as in za-zen, and make sure your chin is drawn in and your neck is also straight. Your line of vision should fall about 2 yards or metres in front of you. Now walk quietly starting with your right foot. Step the length of half your foot and then step with your left foot the length of half a foot (see diagram opposite). Each step is timed to last for one complete breath, that is an inhalation and exhalation. If you have a job coordinating your breathing and walking then just relax, concentrate only on maintaining a good posture and allow the breathing to take care of itself. Slowly you will develop a rhythm between the steps and the breath. If while doing kinhin you meet a wall you turn to the right at a right angle and maintain your pace.

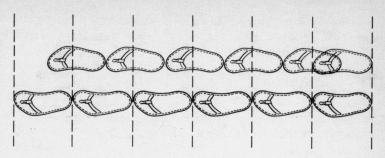

Walking in Kinhin

ZA-ZEN AND KOAN STUDY

Mumon Yamada Roshi said:

Za-zen meditation is the most direct way to the truth of Buddhism. Instead of wandering in thought, you must sit with your whole being, forgetting all intellectual searching. It is said, 'Let one's mind concentrate in silence and let it remain motionless like Mount Sumeru.' If you practise za-zen in this way, you are already in the world of Buddha while among sentient beings. This is called the 'direct entrance into the Buddha stage in one jump.' You have to jump into Buddha's world suddenly. This is why Zen Buddhism is called the 'teaching of sudden awareness' and for this purpose we need za-zen.

There is no existence of Buddha separate from the deluded sentient being. Break through your deluded minds at this very moment and you are Buddha, at this very moment, just as you are. You must cut your dualistic consciousness with thought of unenlightened and enlightened, at its very roots. Doing this you become Buddha.

In order to cut this dualistic consciousness, samadhi power is most necessary. In Zen, to strengthen this samadhi power and break through, we use koans. A koan is an episode of an enlightened person's truthful experience of breaking through. This episode makes it possible for you, by becoming one with the state of mind of the koan, to strengthen your samadhi power. By strengthening your samadhi power and cutting all dualistic consciousness, you can go beyond the dualistic consciousness and experience the same breakthrough that

these episodes express. Doing this, everybody experiences
the same breakthrough that these episodes express. Doing this,
everybody is a Bodhisattva.

The koan system is the unique and traditional teaching method of
the Rinzai school of Zen Buddhism. The koan derive from actual
encounters, usually (but not always) between accomplished Zen
masters and their students. Successive generations of teachers have
related these encounters to their students to illustrate particular principles of Zen. Questions or problems, often paradoxical, highlighted
by each story were presented to students to encourage and test them
in their own training. Over time the encounters and their associated
problems were formalized and systematized into koan collections
like the Mumonkan, the Hekiganroku, the Tetteki Tosui and the
Shoyoroku.

The koan system enables the Zen teacher to test the individual
student's understanding of Zen, not intellectually, but as it applies
to the student's own life. Acting as a focus or catalyst for the student,
it will confront him or her with a challenge the resolution of which
will become of tremendous personal importance and will clarify the
student's understanding of Zen.

Hakuin (1686–1769) said: If you take up one koan and investigate it without ceasing, your thoughts will die and your
ego-demands will be destroyed. It is as though a vast abyss
opened up in front of you, with no place to put your hands
and feet. You face death, and your heart feels as though it
were fire. Then suddenly you are one with the koan, and body
and mind let go. . . . This is known as seeing into one's own
nature. You must push forward relentlessly, and with the help
of this great concentration you will penetrate without fail to
the infinite source of your own nature.

Viewed in mechanical terms, the realization arising from the resolution
of a koan varies from a glimpse of the true Self (like the fractional
exposure to light possible through a camera shutter) to Dai Kensho
itself. But this is very provisional. It is usual for realization through koan
study to mature over time, and whether the teacher sets the student to
work on many koan or only one, none can be fathomed exhaustively.
In fact any experience in koan study that is regarded as an 'attainment',
or in some way final, usually becomes merely a memory through which
the discriminating mind will judge and assess all present and future
experience. The realization then becomes a lifeless burden, preventing

the student from investigating each moment of the mystery of life with an open mind.

Genuine koan study is really only possible under the guidance of a teacher who has him or herself completed the same training. By the indiscriminate selection and study of koan in the absence of a teacher the overwhelming probability is that the would-be student will settle for a very shallow, if not conceptual, resolution of it. For example, reading the koan: 'What was your Original Face before your parents were born?' Many people suppose they must try to imagine how they felt before they were born and embark upon all kinds of visualizations and fantasies in an attempt to recall that experience. Unless they train with a teacher the error of this kind of approach will not become clear.

To appreciate a koan a student must really live with it, or as Hakuin said 'become one with it'. To begin with this can feel artificial, but with determined practice in the face of repeated failure in formal interview with the teacher, the student starts to empathize with the problem the koan represents. It reveals new and different perspectives on the practice of Zen, deepening and clarifying the student's understanding in the process.

THREE ESSENTIAL ELEMENTS OF PRACTICE

Great Faith, Great Doubt and Great Determination have been described as essential to Zen practice, and especially to koan study. They are the dynamics of training.

Great Doubt

A profound sense of doubt, as opposed to mere cynicism or scepticism, is often and ordinarily regarded as a very negative experience which should be denied or ignored. Generally we are encouraged to have a strong sense of who we are, what we do, why we do it, what we like and dislike and so on: and we will go to considerable lengths to maintain that appearance. Thus we may manage our lives through a persona built from a collection of seldom-challenged assumptions, and regard doubt as self-destructiveness or weakness. In fact the very self-destructiveness of doubt is a hint as to its real value, and the real 'weakness' lies in our efforts to evade and dismiss it (behind which there is usually a basic fear of the unknown).

When people first allow themselves to question their lives, the shock is sometimes such that they fear they are going insane: 'And it is true: we are going out of our minds! That is the whole point: to let ourselves go beyond the mind, to stop dwelling in the mind.' (Genpo Merzel Sensei.) Certainly certainty feels more comfortable because it offers a sense of security. But it is prone to become stale and lifeless, whereas doubt admits the possibility of change and renewal. After all, it was doubt about the value of life, its significance in the face of impermanence, that drove Shakyamuni to leave his father's palace and become a wandering mendicant.

Dogen Zenji pointed out:

Impermanence is truly the reality in front of our eyes. We need not wait for some teaching from others, proof from some passage of scripture, or some principle. Born in the morning, dead in the evening, a person we saw yesterday is no longer here today – these are the facts we see with our eyes and hear with our ears. This is what we see and hear about others. Applying this to our own bodies, and thinking of the reality of all things, though we expect to live seventy or eighty years, we die when we must die.

We have seen how acknowledgement of this fact threw Shakyamuni into profound doubt about the worth of the life he had been leading. The koan with which he was forced to wrestle is perhaps the most basic of all: 'What is the meaning of life in the face of inevitable sickness, old age and death?' Dogen Zenji called this the 'Great Matter'. To the extend doubt is denied, and we insist on assumed certainties, we cut ourselves off from the reality of impermanence, thereby avoiding the questions we normally regard as 'religious' or 'philosophical'.

Zen training is not about resolving doubt by formulating intellectual answers to it. Rather, it is concerned with the honest acceptance of doubt as our natural and original state of being. The Korean Zen master Seung Sahn Sunim has called this 'Don't know Mind'. We have already hinted that the certainty of Buddhism is 'Socratic' – Bodhidharma knew that he did not know who he was. Zen practice requires us to surrender into the uncertainty of each moment unconditionally. There is a koan: 'From the top of a hundred foot pole, how do you take one step further?' The point is to give up everything we cling to for security and to surrender into 'don't know mind'; but we must do it endlessly. Thus, although we may acknowledge that we do not know who we are, nor whether we even exist as separate entities, nevertheless something feels, hears, talks and sees. So it is that Dogen Zenji exhorts us:

> There is no way to grasp it. I say to you. Open your hands. Just let everything go, and see. What is body and mind? What are daily activities? What is life and death? Ultimately what are mountains and rivers, the great earth, human beings, animals and dwellings? Take a careful look at these things again and again. By doing so, the dichotomy of movement and stillness is clearly and naturally unborn. However, at this time nothing is fixed. No one can realize this from the human point of view. Many have lost sight of this. People practising Zen! You will attain this first midway on the path. Do not stop practising even after you arrive at the end of the path. That is my wish!

Doubt is uncomfortable for the ego. It undermines everything: jobs, families, friendships, property, spiritual practice; it is indiscriminate. Because it disillusions us, it is also enlightening. However, until we are able to appreciate this it can cause depression, despondency and dejection. Even if we do not feel 'suicidal' we might easily be tempted to give up practice! Shakyamuni passed through this crucial stage when he gave up extreme asceticism. However, he did not give up altogether. He had the faith in himself to acknowledge his failure, and the determination to resolve his doubt by the only means left to him. He sat immovably where he was and confronted life as it manifested in each movement of his own existence as completely and honestly as he could. He practised za-zen.

Great Faith

Without faith in ourselves we cannot live with doubt. The tension between these two is both heightened and resolved through determined practice, therefore Dogen Zenji said:

> Practitioners of the Way must first of all have faith in the Way. Those who have faith in the Buddha-Way must believe that the self is within the Way from the beginning; that you are free from delusive desires, upside-down ways of seeing things, excesses and deficiencies and mistakes. Arousing this kind of faith, clarifying the Way, and practising comprise the foundation of learning the Way.

A lesson a Zen student learns repeatedly is that the source of clinging to the ego mind is the lack of sufficient faith in oneself to let go repeatedly of the one hundred foot pole, continuously taking one step further. The compassionate teacher will keep pushing the student to do this. Through persevering at something it is possible to develop faith in oneself; through Zen training, as one's understanding of the practice matures, that faith becomes gradually less shakeable. In the beginning, however, so long as we are attached firmly to the belief that we are no more than the ego-Self, locked into the physical body, and separated from everyone else, our practice can only be based on strong faith in the Buddha's teachings. We have to believe Shakyamuni, and all the successive masters, when they say each one of us is from the beginningless beginning fully endowed with the wisdom and compassion of the Buddhas. Then we can begin to question: 'If that is so, why can I not see it clearly?' Therefore, with regard to faith, Zen is a religion just like any other. It requires faith in the teaching. However, it is not blind faith and it encourages questioning.

Great Determination

Dogen Zenji said students of the Way should be as keen to practise as they would to extinguish a fire engulfing their hair! Training must be in earnest. Half an hour of dozing on the meditation cushion is just half an hour of dozing. True, during that time the Unborn Buddha-mind is manifesting as a dozing sentient being – but what use is that if the sentient being cannot see it?

There is a tradition in Japan that warriors make good Zen students; when they turned to Zen in medieval times they had no difficulty in grasping the need to train wholeheartedly. Their training was not separate from the rest of their lives. It was a battle, a life-and-death struggle. Between teacher and student in the interview room there often lay the live blade of an unsheathed sword.

The Chinese sage Mencius said:

> When Heaven is about to confer an important office upon a man, it first embitters his heart in its purpose; it causes him to exert his bones and sinews; it makes his body suffer hunger; it inflicts upon him want and poverty and confounds his undertakings. In this way it stimulates his will, steals his nature and thus makes him capable of accomplishing what he otherwise could not have accomplished.

Yasutani Roshi pointed out that although in the practice of both Soto and Rinzai Zen all three elements are present, in the study of koan 'doubt is the main prod to Satori because it allows us no rest'. In Soto practice, however, where koan are not the custom, the element of faith is most prominent: 'We sit in unswerving faith that we are all inherently Buddhas.' The Soto method is not to strive after realization, but to let it well up within us in the way that Suzuki Roshi described becoming wet through during a stroll in the mist (see page 30).

However, Dogen Zenji said that provided each one of us practises with great determination, exclusively and wholeheartedly, ten out of ten will attain the Way.

THE PURPOSE OF ZA-ZEN

Mumon Yamada Roshi said:

'To find the jewel, one must calm the waves; it is hard to find if one stirs up the water. Where the waters of meditation are clear and calm, the mind-jewel will be naturally visible.' Most people would jump into the water if a jewel were dropped into a pond and stir up the water until it becomes too cloudy to find anything but stones or tiles. A wise man would wait for the water to become calm so that the jewel naturally comes to shine by itself. Zen discipline is the same. The more you try to know Zen principles by reading books, the farther you move from Buddha nature. If you try to reach awareness by sitting without wondering, however, the jewel of Buddha-nature will begin to shine by itself; and you will realize the real self for which you have been searching.

Yamada Roshi likened za-zen to settling a pond of muddied, turbulent water. The Unborn is like clear, still water in which the 'jewel' of Enlightenment shines clearly. In this state it reflects everything within it. Like the perfect reflection of the disc of the moon on a calm lake.

Usually our minds bear closest resemblance to a muddy pool, churned up by countless eddies and currents. They are unstable, full of confusion, spinning beyond the control of the will. Yet, often it is only when we first try za-zen and start to count breaths that we notice this. Ordinarily our personal identities are so closely tied up with our thought processes and emotional preoccupations that we do not notice the lack of consistency or cohesion in the way we operate, and we fool ourselves that we are exercising some control over our lives. Through za-zen we see the extent to which this is not so. As our awareness begins to focus on the breath, we discover that we do not have to be consciously involved in all our endless mental activity. In fact, we find that when we do so we are only adding to the turmoil, whereas if we allow thoughts and feelings just to arise and pass, our mental activity begins to subside. Thus, a Soto Zen teacher might say that for example to pursue a koan or count breaths is merely to muddy the waters.

In the Soto Zen school it is usually explained that za-zen is 'jijiyu-zamai' (self-fulfilling; enlightenment-practice as an end-in-itself), or 'Mushotoku' (without thought of gain or goal). The Soto master Taisen Deshimaru said: 'Having even one goal, even the tiniest preference of the most infinitesimal thought, or pursuing some objective, however feeble, automatically and inevitably drives us away from the truth of za-zen.' In Soto Zen it is said that just to sit in the za-zen posture is nothing but the full realization of the Buddha. That is why Nansen told Joshu that the Way is beyond both knowing and not knowing. It is not accomplished by practising from delusion towards Enlightenment. It is simply what is in front of our eyes. However, merely to give up and settle for not knowing is to elect to stay in delusion.

Nansen's point is difficult to understand and if our za-zen consists of what we can only regard as thirty minutes of boredom and irritation in a posture which feels strange and uncomfortable, it is very difficult to appreciate our practice as the full manifestation of the Buddha's Enlightenment. Some people become quite embittered when after a few years of practice they still have not 'realized' anything. Usually they mean that they still cannot appreciate their own za-zen as that of the Buddha. If the accomplishment of the Way is Mushotoku, to the Zen master this concern must seem rather absurd. Nevertheless, beginners and experienced students alike perceive a big difference between their own practice and that of their teachers. It is only natural that they put this down to lack of realization on their part.

Suzuki Roshi, another Soto master, explained: 'Strictly speaking, any effort we make is not good for our practice because it creates waves in our mind. It is impossible, however, to attain absolute calmness of our mind without any effort. We must make some effort, but we must forget ourselves in the effort we make.'

So, if the practice of za-zen as mere mechanical repetition does not work, and if striving towards realization only leads us astray, what should be our aim in za-zen? Yasutani Roshi suggests a threefold inter-connected purpose of za-zen:

1. Joriki (Sanskrit, Samadhi, usually translated as 'concentration').
2. Kensho-godo (awakening to Satori).
3. Mujodo no taigen (actualization of the Buddha Way in daily life).

JORIKI

The first step in za-zen is to develop Joriki, either by counting breaths as has been explained, or by some other method, for example work on a koan or concentrating on maintaining the posture. This brings the attention into appreciation of each moment of experience. By sitting immovably in this way, the mind may settle and awareness expand beyond the narrow preoccupations of the ego and we may experience some of the original harmony between mind, body and nature. As we relax our hold on the opinions of our minds and the tensions within the body, awareness becomes sharp and lucid, the breath calms and deepens. Over time, we begin to develop a strong sense of inner peace and power. Through Joriki we begin to appreciate the relationship between mind and body, and the importance of the za-zen posture. Suzuki Roshi said:

> The position expresses the oneness of duality: not two, and not one . . . Our body and mind are not two and not one. If you think our body and mind are two, that is wrong; if you think they are one that is also wrong, our body and mind are both two *and* one. We usually think that if something is not one, it must be more than one; if it is not singular it is plural. But in actual experience, our life is not only plural, but also singular. Each one of us is both dependent and independent.

To achieve Joriki we do have to practise za-zen and at first it may feel awkward or uncomfortable to keep the spine straight and the knees on the floor. One might even be forgiven for concluding that the postures recommended are specifically designed to promote pain! For most of us when confronted with physical discomfort the mind starts to look for an escape, and the temptation is to fidget or change position. Often we have a low patience threshold where pain is involved, and we live in the expectation that it should not have to be experienced.

However, it seems to be the natural consequence of having a body that any physical position will become uncomfortable if held for long enough. So, whilst there is no reason deliberately to provoke discomfort in our za-zen posture we should not expect to be able to avoid it either.

Unexpectedly, as Joriki develops, discomfort stops being a hindrance to za-zen, and starts to become a friend. Sitting with it, we can push against the 'barrier' set up by the mind against further physical irritation. We start to notice how much of the misery and tension we associate with physical pain is not the result of pain itself but of our attitude towards it. (The same is also true of mental pain. As soon as we stop rejecting it as an experience, and allow it to arise and dissipate just like any other, it ceases to be such a problem.) This idea of pain as a friend may sound masochistic, but actually it is not. We do not persist with painful za-zen just for the sake of it, but rather in order to discover the extent to which the limitations we ordinarily place on our ability to 'cope' are self-imposed. Moreover, as we get used to sitting solidly in za-zen the posture takes on a natural dignity and stillness. One outcome of this is that the pain becomes less and less of a preoccupation. It is best therefore to try to allow ourselves to experience discomfort during za-zen rather than struggle against it. Once we give in and begin to change position it is very difficult to recover our concentration.

By keeping the spine straight and breathing calmly the centre of gravity sinks low into the pit of the stomach. Traditionally this point is called the 'hara', and is located about the width of two fingers below the navel. The hara is said to be the centre of our being, and sometimes people do feel that when Joriki is deep, awareness sinks to this point. The abdomen rises and falls with the breath and the mind-body posture feels relaxed and receptive to sensation without any sense of vulnerability.

As the thought processes begin to slow and attachment to discrimination lessens there is a commensurate increase in our capacity to accept wholeheartedly each and every moment of experience as it arises and passes. Deshimaru Roshi said that when we sit in this way our life is like 'a spring that wells up endlessly fresh. It is always modern, always alive, making itself over again every instant.'

Thus we need to note that to translate Joriki or Samadhi as 'concentration' is not entirely accurate. Further, concentration per se is not, as Suzuki Roshi pointed out, the true purpose of za-zen:

The true purpose is to see things as they are, to observe things as they are, and to let everything go as it goes . . . Zen practice is to open up our small mind. So concentrating is just an aid to help you realize 'big mind', or the mind that is everything. If you want to discover the true meaning of Zen in your everyday life, you have to understand the meaning of keeping your mind on your breathing and your body in the right posture in za-zen. Only in this way can you experience the vital freedom of Zen.

KENSHO-GODO

The next stage in Yasutani Roshi's threefold purpose of Zen is Kensho-godo. Its relationship with Joriki is described by Genpo Merzel Sensei as thus:

When the power of Samadhi is strong enough and we become really stable, when we have completely settled down in breath, mind and body, then any chance event – hearing a bird chirping, seeing a sunset or a flower, looking into another's eyes, stubbing a toe, or getting whacked on the back by a stick – anything can open our eye when we are ready. Once the eye of Prajna (wisdom) is completely open, it can never shut again. But until that happens, its tendency is to close, like the shutter of a camera lens. When it opens a little, we have a small experience, a kensho or glimpse into our true nature, into the essence of mind, the essential aspect of the self. Then we see all dharmas (phenomena) as one, all things as one body; we realize the interdependence of all things.

The first experience of Kensho can be really exhilarating. It can feel as if something has been attained. There is often a feeling of joy and liberation. Yet, as Yasutani Roshi pointed out: 'unless fortified by Joriki, a single experience of Kensho will have no appreciable effect on your life and will fade into a mere memory'.

Once a Kensho becomes a memory the tendency is for us to want to recreate it. To our disappointment though, we find that this is not possible, and the more we try the more dissatisfied we become – always comparing our present experience with the 'big one' we had once before. At this point the practice has to be turned around. That is to say, we cease from striving for Kensho and begin to acknowledge that it was originally fully present. We have only to immerse ourselves in it, in the way that Suzuki Roshi said we become wet through during a walk in the mist. Now we also begin to see that practice and Enlightenment really are one, and the interconnection between Kensho-godo and Mujodo no taigen starts to become clear.

MUJODO NO TAIGEN

Simply by sitting in awareness from moment to moment during za-zen we are perfectly manifesting the realization of the Buddha in our lives. At this stage we can speak of practice for the sake of practice without goal or purpose; we are fully able to appreciate the type of za-zen practice which the Soto school calls 'Shikantaza' (sometimes translated as 'serene reflection'), which means literally 'just to sit', making no effort, in the full realization of the Buddha. This is said to be the purest manifestation of Zen because mind and body are completely forgotten, and we are at complete one with the whole universe.

Suzuki Roshi said:

> Buddha nature is just another name for human nature, our true human nature. Thus even though you do not do anything, you are actually doing something. You are expressing yourself. You are expressing your true nature. Your eyes will express; your voice will express; your demeanour will express. The most important thing is to express your true nature in the simplest, most adequate way and to appreciate it in the smallest existence.'

The point which Yasutani Roshi was keen to make vis-à-vis the purpose of za-zen is that, unless there is Kensho 'you will not directly apprehend the truth of your Buddha nature', not appreciate that just to sit, in choiceless awareness, making no special effort, is the purest expression of it. It is not enough merely to believe that Ordinary Mind is the Way; unless we have Kensho we cannot know the Way for what it is.

5 · FURTHER PRACTICE

Since, at its most basic level, all that is needed for za-zen is a quiet place to sit, anyone can do it at the time and in the place of their choosing, as frequently and for as long as they like. Many people are content to practise in this way and derive considerable benefit from doing so. They find it helps them to relax, to develop self-confidence and concentration. Sometimes, as we have already said, it can be used very effectively to deepen a personal commitment to religious traditions other than Buddhism. This is because za-zen is a universal practice which is completely open-ended. It constantly points us back to our own lives, which must include our own needs and particular cultural conditioning. We will each have our own perspective upon it. As Maezumi Roshi has said:

> To understand one's own self, we definitely cannot live without tradition and without culture. Even if we protest against these things, still we are in them. We are under certain influences one way or another. (In the practice) there is an effort made to find new value in what we have inherited, in accordance with the life we are living.

However, those who decide to practise za-zen regularly, and carry their commitment through, often find that it develops a momentum of its own so that they are drawn towards opportunities to practise for longer and more frequently. Alternatively, they may run into some question or difficulty in relation to practice in respect of which they feel they need some advice. Either way, they begin to search for a teacher, others with whom to practise and information about extended periods of Zen training (usually on Zen meditation retreats or 'Sesshin').

Attending at a Zen centre, or on a sesshin, can feel like a very big and somewhat daunting step. Especially when, in the context of formal training, beginners are confronted with a foreign and bewildering array of ritualistic ways of performing what would otherwise be the simplest of tasks. In Zen generally, but particularly in Soto Zen, there are special procedures for entering and leaving the meditation hall ('Zendo'), sitting down, standing up, bowing, walking, chanting, eating – almost every conceivable daily activity! During a sesshin, the whole day is structured to a routine which does not vary. A typical Sesshin schedule might comprise the following:

4.55	Wake up
5.30–7.45	Za-zen alternated with kinhin
7.45–8.00	Ceremony and chanting
8.00–8.30	Breakfast ceremony ('Oryoki')
9.00–10.30	Retreat centre clean-up/work ('Samu')
11.00	Za-zen
11.30	Dharma talk ('Teisho')
1.10	Ceremony and chanting
1.20	Lunch ceremony ('Oryoki')
1.50–3.30	Rest period/optional za-zen
3.30–5.50	Za-zen and kinhin
5.50	Ceremony and chanting
7.30–9.15	Za-zen and kinhin
9.15	Chanting
10.00	Light out

Note
The meal ceremonies are discussed in Chapter 7 (Zen Food).

In different schools of Zen the schedule may vary in any number of ways. There may be less za-zen and more samu. There may be a third meal, although only breakfast and lunch will be formal. It is not unusual to include yoga, martial arts and other exercises within the schedule, although such classes tend to be optional. Some teachers give 'Dokusan' or 'Sanzen' (private interviews) to their students (this is usual practice in koan study), others prefer the use of public question and answer sessions ('Mondo'). Talks may be more or less formal, and in some systems are given during za-zen itself ('Kusan'). In all cases however the point of the talk is not to convey information, but to bring the listeners to awakening.

It is often a surprise, even a turn off, to some when they find that apart from za-zen so much time is given to ritual.

When we come to Zen practice we inevitably bring all sorts of preconceptions with us. A generally persistent one (which many books encourage, and which is not entirely without foundation) is that Zen is irreligious and iconoclastic. Thus one Western teacher of Zen tells an amusing story about his amazement when, as a beginner, he saw his own teacher bow to a Buddha image. Apparently he told this roshi that he had understood a Zen master would sooner spit at a Buddha image than bow to one. In reply he was told that he could spit if he wished, but the roshi preferred to bow! There is another accomplished Western Zen teacher who, just after he began to practise, was bold enough to tell a Japanese roshi that bowing and ritual are not the true Zen. It was tartly demanded of him what he knew of true Zen. As this confrontation took place in a vegetable plot during samu, the young man picked up a hoe and shook it at the roshi, shouting 'Just this!' With what must have been a withering look the roshi dismissed him: 'Your Dharma eye is not yet open!'

The ritualistic side of Zen is difficult for many people to come to terms with. Yasutani Roshi explained three reasons for ceremony and chanting the sutras:

> The first reason, to make a sincere offering to (the) Buddhist Patriarchs, is a natural expression of gratitude for the opportunity to hear, to believe, to learn and to realize Buddhist teaching.

> Our action in erecting a Buddhist image and offering it incense, flowers, candlelight and deep bows is such an expression. The greatest delight for (the) Buddhist Patriarchs is for their followers to respect, to maintain and to spread the teaching. Therefore, we sit before an image and recite with sincerity the sutras which they composed. In this way, our sutra recitation is the expression of our gratitude to them.

> Second, Buddhist followers want to have others know about and believe and realize the noble teaching of the Buddha . . . we recite sutras before others as an education of their subconscious minds. On the surface, it may seem that (the) effectiveness of teaching is limited by the extent of understanding. So, it may be thought, if we read difficult sutras, they will have no effect. However, only people who do not understand the power and subtlety of the subconscious, hold such an opinion.

If you have studied only a little about the subconscious you will know that even though you do not grasp the meaning with your conscious mind, you may understand very clearly with your subconscious. Or, if you do not get any conscious impression, you may already have a subconscious impression. Moreover, you will know, if you have studied the matter, that our conscious mind is influenced by our subconscious; indeed, that our subconscious operates absolute control over our character. . .

. . . (the) third element is this: if you recite sutras with great energy and single-mindedness frequently, then your own *samadhi-power* will be strengthened and you will have a good chance for *Satori*. Or, if you have already awakened, your *Satori* will shine more brilliantly in your character and act more effectively in your everyday life. The most important attitude in reciting sutras is to recite with your whole spirit.

The tradition in Zen, for everyone to practise together in the same way, reflects the 'oneness and manyness' of realization which Suzuki Roshi called 'Not one; and not two'. It may be understood in various ways.

The word 'Sesshin', for example, means to unite the mind. It refers to the universal mind. It means to bring together and 'become one' with everything that exists, to realize that the whole universe is nothing but the unborn Buddha-mind. We have already seen how the busy conscious mind may be likened to turbulent, muddied waters which can be calmed and cleared through the Joriki of za-zen. All the forms and procedures of Sesshin are designed to carry the Joriki of za-zen into other activities. So that whatever we do becomes our Zen practice, and realization can occur anywhere, not just in za-zen. Therefore Yasutani Roshi said:

If you recite sutras with your whole heart, there will be no difference between za-zen and your recitation.

To take another example, the word 'samu' means 'to wipe out'.

We do not mean just wiping the carpet and the furniture clean, but also wiping mind and self clean. What is all this dirt and dust we clear up? Delusions, defilements – all our opinions and views, me and mine.'

Genpo Merzel Sensei

If we do not have a way to do things on Sesshin, for example how and when to make a full bow, which we learn to do automatically, we start to distract ourselves with all kinds of ideas about when, if and how to do them. Thus Maezumi Roshi has explained:

> Someone says something, we lean toward it and we say: 'That's a very good idea; that's a good way to practise.' And then someone says something else and we say: 'Oh! That's better! Let's do that!' Thus we struggle to make even small decisions. To make our conscious mind function properly is another meaning of Sesshin.

Everyone training together in the same way can look regimented, even somnambulistic, to an outsider, but it is in fact a wonderful opportunity to be free from the need to make so many decisions about how to fill the day. There is no need to discuss, to form opinions, to make choices and so on. Many people find this a tremendous relief, and have much more energy to devote to the practice as a result. When it is time for za-zen, they just get on with za-zen. It is no different when they chant or bow. Training in this way, it does not really matter whether one feels empathy or aversion for the Buddha image on the altar, or anything else. Instead one just participates whole-heartedly in whatever is happening, and the activity of each moment expresses the intimate relationship that exists between everyone and everything, which is implicit in the word 'Sesshin'.

When Sesshin becomes the expression of the unified Buddha-mind, it becomes truly possible to appreciate the seeming contradictions, tensions and conflicts that make up our lives, from a higher level of harmony. The importance of this is emphasized by the Buddhist concept of 'Sangha'. Together with the Buddha and the Dharma, the Sangha is one of the three most precious 'treasures' of Buddhism. In its most literal sense, the Sangha is the Buddhist monastic community. But it is also the collective term for all those engaged in Buddhist practice, at whatever level. Yet again it refers to the harmony within all relationships when appreciated from the perspective of Satori. Such harmony extends to everything that exists. Shakyamuni Buddha acknowledged its universality when Ananda said to him that the Sangha was one half of the Way. The Buddha corrected him. In fact, he said, the Sangha is the whole of the Way. Thus, it may be asked how we can do anything outside of our relationship to our environment and to one another; and in what can the practice of Zen consist, if not in the harmonization of those relationships. Maezumi Roshi has said:

71

Our lives are defined by human relationships. It is nonsense to think of a person existing in isolation. Even if he crawls into a deep mountain there are still connections with others – relatives, friends, parents. You have all sorts of connections with other people. It is like a vast net.

The analogy of the net was developed in the Atvatamsaka Sutra to include not just human beings but the multi-dimensional inter-relationships of the entire cosmos. The Sutra portrays a vast net, symbolizing all that is, each knot of which is a radiant jewel reflecting perfectly, and in microcosm, all the countless other jewels connected to it. The net is in a state of flux, and is forever redefining itself, yet always remaining a harmonious and balanced whole . . .

Just as if each one of us were like a jewel in that net, the teaching of Zen is that everything we are, individually and collectively, affects everything we do, and vice versa. The rituals of Zen Buddhism in whatever form they take, and its insistence on the performance of even the smallest of tasks with great care and attentiveness, may be understood as the expression of the Sangha treasure, the harmony that exists in all things in each moment. So, when people arise from za-zen, for example, they all bow together and begin kinhin, or chanting, according to one procedure. There is a powerful feeling of community and collective endeavour in such shared activity. Prolonged and intensive practice is made much easier by this environment. The atmosphere in the zendo is supportive, and one feels carried along by it.

There is quality to this kind of training which is almost aesthetic, and cognizing the mutually beneficial effect of our practice on one another we can begin to appreciate the nature of Buddhist morality (the precepts) and the law of cause and effect ('Karma'). This is why it is not really correct to say that the practice of Zen is just za-zen; it is 'Kai-Jo-E'. This formulation of the Way, which is as old as Buddha itself, refers to the precepts, Dhyana samadhi (meditation) and wisdom.

So far in this book we have tended to concentrate on samadhi and wisdom. However, we need also to appreciate the precepts since in reality these three aspects of practice cannot be divided up. How the precepts may apply to our everyday lives will be considered in the next chapter. Here we will confine ourselves to the observation that, although ethical behaviour is the result of wisdom which itself derives from samadhi, there can be no samadhi unless we take responsibility for the consequences of our own actions, and see that it is entirely in our own hands to create the right conditions for samadhi to develop. That is precisely what the formal rules of Zen training and our adherence to them are intended to achieve. Nyogen Senzaki said:

> When one keeps the precepts, he can meditate well; when his meditation becomes matured, he attains wisdom. Since these three . . . are interrelated and equally essential, no one of the three can be carried as an independent study.

It is sometimes objected that the traditional training methods are a denial of individual freedom and creativity. In the Far East, on the other hand, there has been no great master of any art who did not spend long years under a teacher learning the rules of that art. The rules provide the fundamental form, or terms of reference, through which the unique and the creative (which arise from complete freedom or mastery within the rules) may be demonstrated and communicated. This has been especially true, for instance, in the art of calligraphy. It will also strike a note with Western students of the martial arts, who are taught to work very hard at perfecting the execution of technique according to a classical pattern. Only when they have mastered the techniques of their arts, are they able to produce genuine originality or innovation. (See Chapter 9. Zen And The Martial Arts.) It is the same in Zen training: in the confines of even the most rigorous and traditional training schedule, the flash of Kensho will always be modern, original and personal.

In fact, the experience of formal Zen training is impossible to convey adequately. During the course of a single period of za-zen, let alone a whole week of Sesshin, one may go through an entire spectrum of mental, emotional and physical responses. It can feel like heaven, it can feel like hell, very often it will feel like both at the same time! But whatever happens to us, we are the ones that are doing it to ourselves, and it is always our own lives which we are encountering. There is a profound intimacy and validity to that experience which it is difficult to find elsewhere. Ultimately that may be what brings people back time and again.

6 · ZEN IN DAILY LIFE

> Until realization manifests itself – in the way we raise a child,
> grow a garden, drive a car, live our life – what the hell good is
> it? Zen has to do with everyday life.
>
> Albert Low

In the East, within the Zen tradition, those Zen students who have
decided to commit themselves fully to self-realization have (at least in
the past) usually become monks or nuns. They give up their worldly
lives and possessions in order to follow their path under the guidance
of a master within the confines of a monastic life.

In the West, Zen is much more of a lay movement and for those
practitioners who wish to maintain their lives both in society and
in the Zen way, a switch of emphasis is necessary. Single minded
devotion to achieving Enlightenment or the 'Great Awakening' has to
give way to a more varied practice in which formal Zen training and
the demands and concerns of ordinary life are interwoven. Together
they can then be used to challenge and test our ability to bring
Zen into our daily lives and to take our life experiences back
to the meditation cushion. The friction generated by this process
can provide the heat that creates the changes through which we
may grow. Unavoidably, this can sometimes be a source of pain
and fear.

Robert Aitken Roshi says that: 'Practice in daily life is the same
practice as on your cushion: check your ordinary thoughts of greed,
hatred and ignorance and return to your original pure mind.' While
the Canadian Zen teacher Albert Low describes the situation as
follows:

One can, by committing oneself fully to the lay life and the sacrifices that it takes, in other words to live fully and authentically the role of a parent and spouse, 'be' committing oneself fully to awakening, to the Dharma. But such a commitment needs constant work, just as commitment to being a monk needs constant work. It is like steering a ship across the ocean; one cannot lash the tiller and then forget about it. It means constantly checking one's course and correcting direction.

In essence Zen is not concerned with how we conduct ourselves in society, but an outcome of Zen teaching is that the dualistic distinction we may make between ourselves and others starts to diminish. This shift in perception is matched by an increased awareness of the interdependence of all phenomena. This then leads to a growing sense of social awareness and community and compassion with other beings. Life itself may then become a koan in which we try to answer the question of how to lead a life that balances our own needs with those of the people and other beings around us.

The realization that you do not exist separately from everything else also carries with it the awareness that you must now accept responsibility not only for the results of your own actions but for everything you experience. It no longer works to say something like, 'she made me jealous'. One must now say 'I made myself jealous'. Now if a problem occurs you cannot look outside of yourself to place the blame but must look inwards, face yourself, and discover what it is in you that engendered a particular situation. To live from this place however requires considerable effort and the ability to stay clear minded within the confusion of our lives. Apart from za-zen and contact with a Zen teacher, practical advice on sustaining ourselves in this endeavour is provided by the Noble Eightfold Path and Ten Precepts of traditional Buddhist teachings combined with the Zen emphasis on 'The Middle Way'.

THE MIDDLE WAY

The Buddha is said to have been radiant, charismatic, gentle and most of all compassionate. His message was a very practical one. He was concerned with showing the way beyond the suffering of existence to a place where one could lead a life of selflessness, compassion and wisdom.

The Buddha's teachings were based on his postulations that

the way to achieve happiness and harmony and the elevation of suffering was to accept the Four Noble Truths and to follow the Noble Eightfold Path.

The Four Noble Truths are:

1. As a result of its impermanence we experience life as suffering;
2. However, suffering itself is caused by our desire for life to be otherwise;
3. Therefore the way to stop suffering is to stop desire;
4. The way to stop desire is to follow the Eightfold Noble Path.

At first sight this seems a most depressing message but the Buddha's teachings offer hope once the fact of suffering has been accepted. That suffering is universal and not the result of accident nor a punishment is illustrated in the Buddha's story of the woman who went to him with her baby, dead in her arms (see page 11).

The Buddha taught that to follow the Eightfold Noble Path was the way to stop desire and the route to spiritual liberation. This path recommends rightness in:

1. understanding,
2. thought,
3. speech,
4. action,
5. livelihood,
6. effort,
7. mindfulness,
8. concentration.

Of course the interpretation of 'rightness' and how it applies to the qualities listed is open to much discussion. This has resulted in various schools of thought but the Zen path recommends the Middle Way with the emphasis on mindfulness cultivated through za-zen. Thus, in Zen, moderation is a quality that is respected. Remember, however, that moderation in moderation is also important, hence the occasional story of Zen masters getting blind drunk! The Middle Way is described as follows by Zen master Gudo Nishijima Roshi:

> The most fundamental teaching of Gautama Buddha is 'Don't do wrong, do that which is right'. So he taught his disciples the eight 'correct ways'. These eight correct paths are all rooted in the balance which one attains through za-zen, that is, the balance between activity and passivity, optimism and pessimism, tension and relaxation, reason and irrationality.
>
> For example, right world view (understanding) refers to

seeing life for what it is and being neither too optimistic nor too pessimistic as a result. Right thinking are those thoughts, plans and theories which arise from a right world view, that is neither too idealistically impractical nor too materialistically trivial. Right speech has often been interpreted as meaning not to tell lies, but in a deeper sense it refers to 'gentle words', speech which is in harmony with both the speaker and listener and their situation. Right action is always appropriate for the situation, and is not unduly influenced by our transient moods or whims. Right livelihood means the correct choice of ways to earn a living. Right effort is the fine work enabled by inner harmony and balance. Right mind, as you may suppose, refers to a tranquil, undisturbed mind. Right body balance refers to being neither too tight nor too loose, neither too tense nor too relaxed.

These goals may seem a bit simple, but, after all, the inspiration for Zen comes from a man like us who lived long ago, and the goal of Zen is to purify and bring ourselves into harmony, not as some fantastic, unbelievable experience, but rather as a return to the good balance we often enjoyed as children. Paradoxically, we can say that the goal of za-zen is, through our effort, to return us to the common place; through hard work to become normal.

This view echoes another Zen master who, when asked for teaching, gave the reply: 'When you bring me a cup of tea, do I not accept it? When you make bows to me, do I not return them? When do I ever neglect to give you teaching? If you want to see, see directly into it; when you try to think about it it is altogether missed.'

MORALITY AND THE TEN PRECEPTS

Do not kill.
Do not steal.
Do not be greedy.
Do not tell a lie.
Do not be ignorant.
Do not talk about others' faults.
Do not elevate yourself by criticizing others.
Do not be stingy.
Do not get angry.
Do not speak ill of the Three Treasures.

These Ten Buddhist Precepts offer us another guideline on how to lead our daily lives but from the Zen point of view they are not necessarily something to be attached to. Rather they offer us an idea of how a deeply enlightened person may behave. They are not commandments in the Christian sense and not to obey them is not a sin, but in Buddhist terms an act of ignorance. They point the way of action towards the discovery of one's own Buddha nature. Philip Kapleau Roshi compares the Precepts to scaffolding; they are needed to erect a large structure but taken down once the building is complete. Thus the enlightened person does not consciously follow the Precepts but he or she will do so spontaneously and naturally as a result of the complete realization of their own Buddha nature. It is perhaps from this perspective that Zen is sometimes described as above morality. Philip Kapleau Roshi says of this:

> Zen transcends morality but does not exclude it. Or to put it more Zen-like, 'Zen is above morality but morality is not below Zen.' The moral man knows right from wrong, or thinks he does, but he does not know who it is who thinks right and wrong. Such deep understanding requires Zen training and awakening.

ZEN AND PSYCHOTHERAPY

Nowadays there is considerable interest on the part of psychotherapists in the connection between psychotherapy and Zen; and the question often arises of whether it is compatible to practise Zen and to be in therapy. For each case this would be for the person's therapist and/or Zen teacher to decide, but a general outline of the similarities and differences between the two might be useful in elucidating the aims of Zen.

Broadly speaking, psychotherapy is about helping us to free ourselves from past, present and future anxieties. It is about being able to function in the world and to manage our affairs and relationships in a relatively satisfactory manner. Therapy requires us to face up to any skeletons we may have lurking in the shadows of the past, to understand and to accept them and thus to reduce the power they may hold over us.

The courage and honesty required to face ourselves in this way is also a pre-requisite of Zen practice and at this level there is a relationship between Zen and psychotherapy. However, the aspiration of the Zen student goes further than the wish to be a well-rounded person managing their lives in the world. The Zen practitioner wishes to move on from this plane of firm ego strength to one where the ego and the personal self are transcended. He or she wishes to experience the source from which human consciousness arises and to live out of this very ground of being. The question is now no longer 'I' focused but it is instead 'Who am I?'.

On the way to answering this question and afterwards we (Zen students) need, however, to bring Zen back into our daily lives. Here psychotherapy may help with our Zen practice. The nature of Zen practice will lead us to demonstrate more compassion for our families, colleagues, employees, bosses and all the people we meet in our daily round. If psychotherapy can help us in this endeavour then it can work with the Way of Zen.

ZEN AND COUPLES

It is not uncommon that one partner in a couple becomes interested in Zen while the other does not. This can be a source of difficulty and division within the relationship. The uninvolved partner may understandably feel excluded and threatened by their spouse or friend practising meditation behind a closed door and 'getting involved in a strange foreign "religion"'.

To prevent this type of situation developing it is a good idea for us to be open from the beginning about our interest in Zen. We need to explain as best we can what it is about for us and why we are interested. Perhaps we should also mention that the essence of the practice is not to escape from ourselves but to accept self responsibility and to care for those around us. We need to try not to let za-zen time be at the expense of family or relationship time even if this requires getting up earlier or giving up some other pastime. It is a good idea as well not to be self-conscious or secretive about meditation. It is an ordinary thing to do. Children at least initially may also wish to see what we are up to. A good idea is to invite them into the meditation room on the condition that they sit down and do not chatter and that they can leave quietly whenever they wish to.

Finally, the very best way we can receive support in our practice is for those around us to feel as though they are benefiting from possible changes in our behaviour towards them.

ENGAGED BUDDHISM

Once upon a time there was a bed of squashes ripening in the corner of a field. One day they began quarrelling. The squashes split up into factions and made a lot of noise shouting at one another. The head priest of a nearby temple, hearing the sound, rushed out to see what was wrong. He scolded the wrangling squashes saying 'Whatever are you doing. Fighting among yourselves is useless. Every one do za-zen!'

The priest taught them all how to sit properly in za-zen and gradually their anger died away. Then the priest said, 'Put your hands on top of your heads.' The squashes did so and discovered a peculiar thing. Each one had a stem growing from its head which connected them all one to another and back to a common root. 'What a mistake we have made!' they said, 'We are all joined to one another, based on the same root and living one life only. In spite of that we quarrel. How foolish our ignorance has been.'

Kosho Uchiyami Roshi

Like the squashes, Zen practice leads us to a recognition of the interdependence of all life. For some people this awareness carries with it a wish or sense of obligation to go out into the world to try to remedy some of the many examples of social inequality that we see around us and on the news every night. Others feel that they cannot hope to help others without first gaining a substantial degree of self knowledge themselves. They are wary that social concern may be a camouflage for satisfying one's own needs for self affirmation or social or political power and thus just another way of inflating the ego. The controversy between both points of view has been raging in the Buddhist world for many years and both sides can produce very convincing arguments to support their opposing cases. Perhaps the best we can do is to move slowly from egoistic self assertion to a place where our giving is less selfish and finally to the stage where we may give with no thought of self or do-gooding. Here we give because it is the natural thing to do. Along the way we will have to make up our own minds about when the time is right to concentrate on inner work and when we need to act to help alleviate social injustice.

7 · ZEN FOOD

As with other spiritual paths correct food preparation and good dietary practice form an integral part of Zen training. The philosophy of food preparation in a Zen temple is encapsulated in the style of cooking called *shojin ryori*. This may be simply translated as 'vegetable cooking', but *shojin ryori* carries with it the idea of cooking for spiritual development and its purpose is to contribute to the physical, mental and spiritual health of the cook and those who partake of the food.

In Japanese the word *shojin* is composed of the characters for 'spirit' and 'to progress' and the complete meaning of the word is something like 'dedication in progressing along the path to salvation'. The Chinese word from which shojin was derived was itself a derivative of the Sanskrit term *virya* which contains within it the idea of both total effort and self control, two qualities which are elemental in the Buddhist Eightfold Noble Path. However, the underlying principle of shojin ryori is the very simple one of love and gratitude for the food received. Preparing and partaking of food becomes part of religious practice and takes its place alongside other contributions to the happiness and welfare of society and ourselves.

Shojin cookery had its origins in China and the philosophy underlying it was taken back to Japan by monks who had been to China to study Ch'an. One of the most famous of these was Dogen Zenji who wrote two treatises on the subject: *A Guide for the Kitchen Supervisor* and *Instructions for the Zen Cook*. They became reference works in many Zen monasteries and the principles extolled also influenced more general developments in Japanese cooking. A number of the unique characteristics of traditional Japanese cuisine have their origins in shojin ryori.

In his book *Instructions for the Zen Cook* (Tenzo Kyokun), Dogen carefully explains the qualities to look for in choosing the cook or tenzo for monastery duties. He says 'Tenzo duty is awarded only to those of excellence who exhibit faith in Buddhist teachings, have a wealth of experience and possess a righteous and benevolent heart. This is because tenzo duty involves the whole person.' Further he says that if a person entrusted with the job of tenzo lacks such qualities or the spirit for the job, then they will endure unnecessary hardships and suffering and the work will have no value in their pursuit of the way. The job of cook as far as Dogen is concerned is obviously a serious one.

The same sentiment is expressed by the Chinese monk Zongze (AD 1102) who wrote a ten volume work called *Regulations for Zen Monasteries* (in Chinese, Chanyuan Qinggui, or Zen'en Shingi in Japanese). Ten volumes! He tells the tenzo to 'put your awakened mind to work making a constant effort to serve meals full of variety that are appropriate to the need and the occasion, and that will enable everyone to practise with their bodies and minds with the least hindrance.' (See *Refining Your Life*, translation by Thomas Wright, Wetherhill 1983.)

Of course preparing food in the frame of mind recommended by Dogen and Zongze is an extremely difficult task and it requires the cook to be totally present for the job. Perhaps giving all our attention to the simplest tasks is the wisest way to start, 'when washing rice focus attention on the washing and let no distraction enter'.

In her book *Good Food from a Japanese Temple* (Kodansha International, Tokyo, 1982) Soei Yoneda, Abbess of Sanko-in Temple describes the Zen cook's job in very practical terms thus:

> It is imperative for the tenzo to actively involve himself person-
> ally in both the selection and the preparation of ingredients.
>
> The tenzo also inspects the rice as it is washed in order to
> ensure the absence of sand or grit. This he carefully discards,
> but not without being on constant guard for even one grain of
> rice that might be mistakenly wasted. He at no time lets his
> mind wander as he cleans the rice. The tenzo also concerns
> himself with the 'six tastes' and the 'three virtues' (rokumi
> santoku). The six tastes are bitter, sour, sweet, hot, salty and
> 'delicate' (ewai), and the tenzo works to balance these effec-
> tively, while also incorporating the three virtues of lightness

and softness, cleanliness and freshness, and precision and care. In so doing, he expresses the spirit of shojin cookery. A balance of the six tastes and the three virtues happens naturally when, in the cleaning of the rice, the washing of the vegetables, the boiling in the pot, and in all the other aspects of the cooking process, the tenzo commits himself totally and directs his attention to nothing else but the work at hand.

Shojin cookery is also sometimes referred to as *yukuseki* or medicine. This embodies the same principle as that contained in the Indian ayurvedic medical system. In this school of thought food selection and preparation are seen to be inseparable from the treatment of disease and the cultivation of good health. The traditional Chinese medical view is the same thus, 'If one falls ill one should first examine one's diet, then choose well, chew carefully and give thanks. In this way the curative powers of nature with which mankind is blessed are given full rein to act and nearly all diseases are conquered.'

The Zen diet is traditionally vegetarian and a practitioner abstains from eating all flesh foods, except in particular defined circumstances. This vegetarian practice is based on the Buddhist precept of non-killing of all sentient beings which recognizes the interdependency and oneness of all life. For a detailed argument against eating flesh foods see *A Buddhist Case For Vegetarianism* by Roshi Philip Kapleau, Rider & Co. Ltd, London 1983.

Another characteristic of shojin cookery is that no food should be wasted and even such things as vegetable parings are made use of. The Zen cook thus needs to be skilled at both planning and cooking a meal and at utilizing all the scraps. According to Dogen the cook should calculate down to a grain of rice how much food will be needed.

Before each meal the Zen practitioner recites a Sutra. There are different ones for different times of the day or season or particular occasion but the *Gokan no be* or Five Reflections Before Eating is heard at most meals. *Gokan no be* is chanted in a variety of forms but they all have the same message. Here is the version we are familiar with, for lunch time:

LEADER   We offer this meal of three virtues and six tastes to the Buddha, Dharma, and Sangha and to all the life in the Dharma worlds.

ALL   First, seventy-two labours brought us this food; we should know how it comes to us. Second, as we receive this offering, we should consider whether our virtue and practice deserve it.

Third, as we desire the natural order of mind to be free from clinging, we must be free from greed.

Fourth, to support our life we take this food. Fifth, to attain our Way we take this food.

The Sutra is recited to remind and renew the understanding of the partakers of the food of the path of the Buddha.

The first line reminds us of how much effort by very many people went into growing, harvesting, processing, cooking and serving the food about to be eaten and how food may only be grown because of the natural gifts of sunshine, rain and soil.

The second line asks if we have acted with enough charity, love and effort at good practice to deserve such a gift.

The third line reminds us not to be greedy and to remember in not eating overmuch those people who are hungry.

The fourth line expresses the view discussed previously that food is a medicine needed to sustain physical and spiritual strength.

Finally, the fifth line reminds us that we eat to be given the opportunity to follow the Buddha Way and to express our Buddhahood in the world.

8 · THE OX-HERDING PICTURES

The path of Zen has been written about in many different ways but one of the most helpful ways for understanding its essence is through the pictorial representation of the Ox-herding Pictures. These are a series of drawings which tell the story of the stages passed through by a Zen practitioner as he searches for, finds and then lives according to his true nature. In the pictures the ox represents Buddha nature or one's true self and the ox herd, the human being. The paths charted by the drawings are perhaps analogous to the levels of spiritual development also described by Christian mystics. The pictures have been used to illustrate Zen teachings ever since they were produced during the Sung dynasty in China. There are a number of versions of them along with associated interpretations, commentaries and poems. The best known stem from the Chinese Ch'an (Zen) master K'uo-an Chih-yuan. A translation of his words by D.T. Suzuki with woodcut prints by Tomikichiro Tokuriti is given here. The stages depicted are:

1. seeking the ox;
2. finding the tracks;
3. first glimpse of the ox;
4. catching the ox;
5. taming the ox;
6. riding the ox home;
7. ox forgotten, self alone;
8. both ox and self forgotten;

9. returning to the source;
10. entering the market place with helping hands.

The drawing, poem and commentary for each stage are followed for interest by a brief interpretation of the drawing's meaning extracted from the book *The Inward Arc*, Frances Vaughan, Shambhala, 1986. The book is subtitled *Healing and Wholeness in Psychotherapy and Spirituality*, and the comments provide a fascinating link between traditional Zen thought and contemporary spiritual/psychotherapeutic ideas.

1. SEARCHING FOR THE OX

The beast has never gone astray, and what is the use of searching for him? The reason why the oxherd is not on intimate terms with him is because the oxherd himself has violated his own inmost nature. The beast is lost, for the oxherd has himself been led out of the way through his deluding senses. His home is receding farther away from him, and byways and crossways are ever confused. Desire for gain and fear of loss burn like fire; ideas of right and wrong shoot up like a phalanx.

Alone in the wilderness, lost in the jungle, the boy is searching,
  searching!
The swelling waters, the far-away mountains, and the unend-
  ing path;
Exhausted and in despair, he knows not where to go,
He only hears the evening cicadas singing in the maple-woods.

The first ox-herding picture marks the beginning of the inward arc or the spiritual path. The person has become aware of the possibility of enlightenment, and sets out to look for it. Having realized that the external world will never give lasting satisfaction, the seeker turns attention to consciousness. At this point the seeker is likely to be confused by the maze of paths purported to be the way to liberation. Every path seems to say 'Follow me if you want to find yourself, be free from suffering, and attain enlightenment.' A sense of exhilaration and excitement often accompanies the change in values when worldly desires are placed by spiritual ambition.

2. SEEING THE TRACES

By the aid of the sutras and by inquiring into the doctrines, he has come to understand something, he has found the traces. He now knows that vessels, however varied, are all of gold, and that the objective world is a reflection of the Self. Yet, he is unable to distinguish what is good from what is not, his mind is still confused as to truth and falsehood. As he has not yet entered the gate, he is provisionally said to have noticed the traces.

By the stream and under the trees, scattered are the traces of
   the lost;

The sweet-scented grasses are growing thick – did he find
the way?
However remote over the hills and far away the beast may
wander,
His nose reaches the heavens and none can conceal it.

The second ox-herding picture represents the seeker who has begun
to study the wisdom teachings – in this case, Buddhism. This stage
in the quest involves intellectual knowledge. The seeker becomes a
serious student and may feel certain that he or she has found the
right path.

3. SEEING THE OX

The boy finds the way by the sound he hears; he sees thereby into
the origin of things, and all his senses are in harmonious order. In
all his activities, it is manifestly present. It is like the salt in water
and the glue in colour. (It is there though not distinguishable as an
individual entity.) When the eye is properly directed, he will find
that it is no other than himself.

On a yonder branch perches a nightingale cheerfully singing;
The sun is warm, and a soothing breeze blows, on the bank the
willows are green;

The ox is there all by himself, nowhere is he to hide himself;
The splendid head decorated with stately horns – what painter
    can reproduce him?

The third ox-herding picture represents a shift of attention from esoteric teachings to direct experience. The source is found to be present in everyday sounds and activities, and in the six senses. The student at this stage has become a practitioner who is consciously enlightened, no longer seeking or following tracks. The ox is known to be all paths, as well as the seeker and forest itself. This is a stage of insight which requires further discipline for stabilization. Enlightenment has been glimpsed but requires further work to be developed into an abiding light.

4. CATCHING THE OX

Lost long in the wilderness, the boy has at last found the ox and his hands are on him. But, owing to the overwhelming pressure of the outside world, the ox is hard to keep under control. He constantly longs for the old sweet-scented field. The wild nature is still unruly, and altogether refuses to be broken. If the oxherd wishes to see the ox completely in harmony with himself, he is surely to use the whip freely.

> With the energy of his whole being, the boy has at last taken
> hold of the ox:
> But how wild his will, how ungovernable his power!
> At times he struts up a plateau,
> When lo! he is lost again in a misty unpenetrable mountain-
> pass.

In the fourth ox-herding picture the ox is stubborn and unbridled, and
filled with wild strength. The practitioner must practise self-discipline
in every aspect of life. The release of energy at this stage can be both
creative and destructive. Containment is necessary, and the practitioner
is advised to practise truthfulness, compassion, and non-violence.

5. HERDING THE OX

When a thought moves, another follows, and then another – an
endless train of thoughts is thus awakened. Through enlightenment
all this turns into truth; but falsehood asserts itself when confusion
prevails. Things oppress us not because of an objective world, but
because of a self-deceiving mind. Do not let the nose-string loose,
hold it tight, and allow no vacillation.

> The boy is not to separate himself with his whip and tether,
> Lest the animal should wander away into a world of defilements;
> When he is properly tended to, he will grow pure and docile;

Without a chain, nothing binding, he will by himself follow
the oxherd.

The fifth ox-herding picture is a stage of advanced training in
which an effortless friendship is established with one's own true
nature. The advanced practitioner lets go of disciplines learned at
an earlier stage, and even the discriminations between truth and
illusion are transcended. Discrimination between spiritual life and
ordinary life is no longer useful, and one makes friends with the
limitations of ego. The ox becomes a free companion, and movement
is balanced.

6. COMING HOME ON THE OX'S BACK

The struggle is over; gain and loss, the man is no more concerned
with. He hums a rustic tune of the woodman, he sings simple
songs of the village-boy. Saddling himself on the ox's back, his
eyes are fixed at things not of the earth, earthy. Even if he is
called, he will not turn his head; however enticed he will no more
be kept back.

Riding on the animal, he leisurely wends his way home;
Enveloped in the evening mist, how tunefully the flute vanishes
away!

91

Singing a ditty, beating time, his heart is filled with a joy
  indescribable!
That he is now one of those who know, need it be told?

This drawing depicts the sage riding easily on the ox. 'The struggle is
over, "gain" and "loss" no longer affect him.' At this stage the sage radiates enlightenment, and actions are characterized by simplicity, naturalness, spontaneity, and tranquillity. The sage blends with the ordinary
flow of life, but the subtle illusion of the ox as a separate entity persists.

7. THE OX FORGOTTEN, LEAVING THE MAN ALONE

The dharmas are one and the ox is symbolic. When you know that
what you need is not the snare or set-net but the hare or fish; it is
like gold separated from the dross, it is like the moon rising out of
the clouds. The one ray of light serene and penetrating shines even
before days of creation.

Riding on the animal, he is at last back in his home,
Where lo! the ox is no more; the man alone sits serenely.
Though the red sun is high up in the sky, he is still quietly
  dreaming,
Under a straw-thatched roof are his whip and rope idly lying.

In the seventh ox-herding picture, the two have become one. The
seeker has returned home. The sage now regards Self as the full

expression of true nature, and no longer needs concepts or practice. Solitude and serenity are enjoyed in the absence of distinctions.

8. THE OX AND THE MAN BOTH GONE OUT OF SIGHT

All confusion is set aside, and serenity alone prevails; even the idea of holiness does not obtain. He does not linger about where the Buddha is, and as to where there is no Buddha he speedily passes by. When there exists no form of dualism, even a thousand-eyed one fails to detect a loop-hole. A holiness before which birds offer flowers is but a farce.

> All is empty – the whip, the rope, the man, and the ox:
> Who can ever survey the vastness of heaven?
> Over the furnace burning ablaze, not a flake of snow can fall:
> When this state of things obtains, manifest is the spirit of the
> ancient master.

The eighth ox-herding picture, an open circle, is associated with the *dharmakaya*, the causal realm in which consciousness remembers its prior unity as no-thing. There are no theories or holders of theory in the dharmakaya. Illusory barriers have evaporated, and a profound state of emptiness is open to the fullness of life. The idea of enlightenment itself is transcended. Individual consciousness disappears into that from which it originally sprang.

9. RETURNING TO THE ORIGIN, BACK TO THE SOURCE

From the very beginning, pure and immaculate, the man has never been affected by defilement. He watches the growth of things, while himself abiding in the immovable serenity of non-assertion. He does not identify himself with the māyā-like transformations (that are going on about him), nor has he any use of himself (which is artificiality). The waters are blue, the mountains are green; sitting alone, he observes things undergoing changes.

> To return to the Origin, to be back at the Source – already a
>   false step this!
> Far better it is to stay home, blind and deaf, and without
>   much ado;
> Sitting in the hut, he takes no cognizance of things outside,
> Behold the streams flowing – whither nobody knows; and the
>   flowers vividly red – for whom are they?

In the ninth ox-herding picture formless awareness grows back into form without losing its formlessness. It was necessary for form to dissolve into emptiness before it could become the source. Now emptiness melts into spring. There is no need to strive. Everything is observed to be endlessly changing.

10. ENTERING THE CITY WITH BLISS-BESTOWING HANDS

His thatched cottage gate is closed, and even the wisest know him not. No glimpses of his inner life are to be caught; for he goes on his own way without following the steps of the ancient sages. Carrying a gourd[1] he goes out into the market, leaning against a staff[2] he comes home. He is found in company with wine-bibbers and butchers, he and they are all converted into Buddhas.

Bare-chested and bare-footed, he comes out into the market-
place;
Daubed with mud and ashes, how broadly he smiles!
There is no need for the miraculous power of the gods,
For he touches, and lo! the dead trees are in full bloom.

The tenth ox-herding picture obliterates oneness as well as twoness. Here the sage is depicted returning to the human world of everyday life as a bodhisattva, one who has renounced personal liberation to help others. Open hands represent perfect emptiness, and no attempt is made to follow earlier sages. The enlightened one cheerfully manifests enlightenment and follows no path.

[1] Symbol of emptiness (sūnyatā).
[2] No extra property he has, for he knows that the desire to possess is the curse of human life.

95

9 · ZEN AND THE MARTIAL ARTS

To appreciate the influence that Zen has had on the martial arts it is necessary first to look at the men who practised the martial arts as a profession. The word 'samurai' means 'those who serve' and it was first used between the ninth and eleventh centuries AD to describe the armed retainers of powerful Japanese landowners. Between the eleventh and seventeenth centuries Japan experienced an almost continuous series of civil wars as various clans, generals and emperors vied for dominance.

The samurai's role was simple; his obligation was to fight and if necessary die for his lord. Experience taught him that a fight has only three possible outcomes:

- death
- mutual death or injury
- victory

Anything which could increase his chances of survival was of great interest. Improved weapons and armour were developed; fighting techniques were systematically taught by professional instructors who developed their own ryu or traditions, and methods of psychological and spiritual preparation were investigated. It was in the area of psychological preparation that Zen was found to be of value.

In the twelfth century two powerful clans, the Taira and the Minamoto, fought a series of battles culminating in the Gempai War (1180–1185). The Minamoto emerged as the de facto rulers of

Japan, organizing a new form of military government headed by a dictator who took the title of Shogun. The Emperors, based in Kyoto, lacked the military power to rule effectively, and the Shogun, based in Kamakura, allowed the Emperor to survive only as a figurehead, while actual power was retained in the hands of the samurai.

Buddhism officially entered Japan in AD 552 when the Emperor Kimmei (reigned AD 539–572) received a bronze statue of Shakyamuni and some Buddhist sutras from the King of Kudara, a small kingdom in Korea. Various different schools of Buddhism became established, and in the Kamakura period (1192–1333) Zen was introduced into Japan from the Chinese mainland. Japanese priests (such as Eisai and Dogen) studied Zen in China and returned to Japan to promote its teachings. Chinese priests also travelled to Japan; one of whom, Bukko Kokushi (1226–1286), the National Teacher, taught Zen to Hojo Tokimune (1251–1284), who was then the Shogun.

Zen appealed to the military classes for a number of reasons. It was a method which valued direct experience over intellectual speculation and encouraged the development of a courageous, self reliant, ascetic personality, all attributes which a warrior would find attractive.

In November 1274 the Mongol invasion fleet set sail for Japan. Tokimune went to see his teacher Bukko and said:

'The greatest event of my life is at last here.'
Bukko asked, 'How would you face it?'
Tokimune shouted 'Katsu!' as if he were frightening away all his enemies actually before him.
Bukko was pleased and said: 'Truly, a lion's child roars like a lion!'

History records that the Mongol invasion failed due to the effects of a terrible storm and the spirited resistance put up by the samurai.

Bukko, Tokimune's teacher, had himself shown commendable bravery and spiritual strength in the face of death. When the Mongols invaded China, a detachment of Mongol troops entered the Noninji temple where Bukko lived. As he sat in za-zen meditation he recited a poem as the Mongols drew their swords:

In heaven and earth, no crack to hide;
Joy to know that man is void and the things too are void.
Splendid the great Mongolian longsword,
Its lightning flash cuts the spring breeze.

T. Leggett – *Zen and the Ways*, p. 64

The Mongols, perhaps impressed by Bukko's lack of fear, left him unharmed. Obviously the ability to maintain a calm and ordered mind in the face of death was of great use to the samurai, and so in the Kamakura area a form of Zen known as Warrior Zen arose. As the samurai were unlikely to be familiar with the classical texts and stories of Chinese Buddhism a method known as Shikin Zen (on the instant Zen) arose in which the koans they used were derived from the every day experience of the samurai rather than classical Chinese tales.

While the samurai may have initially been attracted to Zen for limited practical purposes, there is no doubt that for many Zen led them to spiritual maturity. When Tokimune died at the age of thirty-three, in 1284, his teacher Bukko said that he had been a Bodhisattva and had ruled for twenty years without joy or anger; having looked for the truth of Buddhism he had found Enlightenment.

From Kamakura, Zen spread all over Japan and large temples were opened in Kyoto. The Imperial family gave their support to various Japanese Zen masters as did the Shoguns and their samurai supporters, and in time a distinctive Japanese form of Zen arose in which classical koans were only introduced after progress had already been made with za-zen and simpler koans.

Towards the end of the sixteenth century, Takeda Shingen (1521–1573) and Uyesugi Kenshin (1530–1578) were rival generals in the unceasing power struggle that had plagued Japan for centuries. They were both followers of Zen and although rivals, showed a surprising degree of chivalry and courtesy towards one another. One famous story illustrates their Zen-influenced behaviour. During one of the battles at Kawanakajima, Kenshin rode directly into Shingen's camp. He drew his sword and held it above Shingen's head, saying, 'What do you say at this moment?' Shingen calmly answered 'A snowflake on the hot stove', simultaneously deflecting the sword with his tessen or iron war fan.

Although both Takeda Shingen and Uyesugi Kenshin lived through some very violent times and were professional soldiers their early education in Buddhist monasteries and their later study under Zen masters meant that they grew up to be cultured and civilized men, as well versed in the arts of peace as of war.

In 1600 a great battle took place at Sekigahara. The result was that the Tokugawa family came to power and imposed peace on Japan for almost three centuries. The samurai gradually changed from warriors to administrators and bureaucrats and the aim of the martial arts also began to change; instead of training for death on the battlefield, the samurai began to use the martial arts as paths towards spiritual growth. Swordsmanship, which was considered to be the epitome of the martial arts, became a vehicle for spiritual training, a method in which the sword is changed from an instrument that takes life, satsujin no ken, to something which gives life, katsujin no ken.

The third Tokugawa Shogun, Iyemitsu (1604–1651) studied swordsmanship from Yagyu Tajima no kami Munenori (1571–1646). Yagyu Munenori was a follower of the Zen master Takuan Soho (1573–1645), and included much of Takuan's teachings in his work the *Heihokadensho* which deals to a large extent with the state of the swordsman's mind rather than technique:

> In Zen Buddhism there is the phrase 'Great function clearly manifest knows no rules'. 'Clearly manifest' means that the Great Function of a man of Great Potential appears right before one's eyes. 'Knows no rules' means that a man of Great Potential and Great Function does not adhere to practice and drills. 'Rules' means practice, drills and regulations. In all disciplines there is practice, rules, and regulations, but the man who has reached the deepest principle of his discipline can dispense with them as he pleases. This is complete freedom, and a man of Great Potential and Great Function has a freedom beyond the rules.
>
> *Heihokadensho* translated by William Scott Wilson

According to Yagyu Munenori the last stage in the art of the sword is to be of 'no mind' (mushin), a state in which the swordsman transcends feelings of fear or pride, his ego does not interfere with the spontaneous free play of the sword. His mental state is that of his everyday mind (heijo-shin), a state of being aware of what is happening without attaching or clinging to anything. This echoes the teaching of the Zen master Huang-Po in the *Treatise on the Essentials of the Transmission of Mind* where he says:

> When a mind is free from all form, it sees into (the fact) that there is no distinction between Buddhas and sentient beings; when once this state of mushin is attained it completes the Buddhist life.

Takuan wrote a long letter to Yagyu Munenori known as the *Fudochishinmyoroku* (The Mysterious Record of Immovable Wisdom), which offered him advice on how to train his mind in order to improve his art. He warns against the mind 'stopping' during a fight:

In the practice of Buddhism, there are said to be fifty-two stages, and within these fifty-two, the place where the mind stops at one thing is called the abiding place. Abiding signifies stopping, and stopping means the mind is being detained by some matter, which may be any matter at all.

To speak in terms of your own martial art, when you first notice the sword that is moving to strike you, if you think of meeting that sword just as it is, your mind will stop at the sword in just that position, your own movements will be undone, and you will be cut down by your opponent. This is what stopping means.

Takuan goes on to say that if the swordsman's mind does not stop and the response can be instantaneous then the 'sword that was going to cut you down will become your own, and contrarily, will be the sword that cuts down your opponent.'

The perfect result flows naturally from a mind clear of delusion: like the moon reflected in a stream, the water may be turbulent but the moon remains serene.

By the middle of the eighteenth century some swordsmen had come to reject the idea of fighting altogether. A Kenjutsu (sword-art) master named Kimura Kyuho wrote the *Kenjutsu Fushiki Hen* (The Unknown Art of Swordsmanship) in 1768. He says:

The perfect swordsman avoids quarrelling or fighting. Fighting means killing. How can one human being bring himself to kill a fellow being? We are all meant to love one another and not to kill ... The sword is an inauspicious instrument to kill in some unavoidable circumstances. When it is to be used, therefore, it ought to be the sword that gives life and not the sword that kills.

In the second half of the nineteenth century Japan went through a dramatic process of change. The Emperor was restored to power, the samurai ceased to exist as a class and the country was opened to Western science and technology. Strangely at this time of change there lived an individual who perhaps best exemplifies the traditional Zen derived art of swordsmanship. Yamaoka Tesshu was born in 1836 to a family of high ranking Tokugawa samurai. At the age of eleven he began to study the martial arts and also Zen which his father believed would help him to develop fudo-shin, the immovable mind much admired by the samurai. In 1853 Tesshu entered the Kobukan Military Institute and the Yamaoka Ryu (school) of so-jutsu (spear fighting). He married into the Yamaoka family in 1855 and continued his training. He had been introduced to swordsmanship by the Shinkage Ryu master Kasumi Kantekisai and for the rest of his life trained with so much determination and ferocity that he was nicknamed 'Demon Tetsu' (Tetsu was his earlier name, later changed to Tesshu). Although he defeated almost everyone he faced, he could never overcome Asari Gimei, a master swordsman of the Nakanishi-ha Itto Ryu. He went to Tekisui, the abbot of Tenryuji, who gave Tesshu the following koan to solve:

> When two flashing swords meet there is no place to escape;
> Move on coolly, like a lotus flower blooming in the midst of a
>   roaring fire,
> And forcefully pierce the Heavens!
>
> *The Sword of No-Sword* by John Stevens

After struggling with this koan and driving himself through many sessions of hard training Tesshu achieved his enlightenment. He went to Asari to put his new awareness to the test, but as soon as they crossed *swords*, Asari dropped his blade, announcing, 'You have arrived!'

After this breakthrough Tesshu established his Muto Ryu (No Sword School). He opened a dojo, the Shumpukan, where he began to teach his own disciples. One advanced training method involved facing hundreds of opponents day after day for up to seven days. One candidate, Kagawa Zenjiro, left a record of his experiences. By the end of the third day he was physically exhausted; his hands were cracked and bleeding from holding the sword, and he was barely able to stand. He explains what happened when he faced an opponent noted for foul play:

> When I saw him coming up to me, I made up my mind that this would be my last combat, for I might not survive the contest. With this determination I felt within myself the surging up of a new energy. I was quite a different person. My sword returned to its proper position. I approached him now fully conscious of my fresh inner surge and lifting up the sword over my head, was ready to strike him with one blow of it. At this moment came the master's emphatic command to stop, and I dropped my sword.

Tesshu stopped the match because he realized that Kagawa had achieved a breakthrough and had realized the 'sword of no sword'.

Perhaps the first Westerner to have had direct experience of a Zen influenced training in the martial arts was the German Eugen Herrigel who studied Kyudo (archery) under Master Awa (1880–1939) from 1932–1937. In his book *Zen in the Art of Archery* Herrigel says that:

> The art of archery is rather like a preparatory school for Zen, for it enables the beginner to gain a clearer view, through the work of his own hands, of events which are not in themselves intelligible.

Herrigel's training was severe. He was made to practise drawing the bow and releasing the arrow constantly: hitting the target was not important, Master Awa constantly stressed that Herrigel's mental state was all. He had to achieve an ego-less state in order to make any progress. Finally Herrigel asked:

> 'How can the shot be loosed if "I" do not do it?'
> '"It" shoots', he replied.
> 'I have heard you say that several times before, so let me put it another way: How can I wait self-obliviously for the shot if "I" am no longer there?'
> '"It" waits at the highest tension.'
> 'And who or what is this "I"?'
> 'Once you have understood that, you will have no further need of me. And if I tried to give you a clue at the cost of your own experience, I should be the worst of teachers and should deserve to be sacked! So let's stop talking about it and go on practising.'

Eventually Herrigel achieved mastery, or in Master Awa's words, he became the 'Master of the artless art'.

Nowadays, the martial arts are often simply practised as competitive sports. However the Zen approach can still be found in Japan and other countries. In 1972 the Chozen-Ji Zen temple was established in Kalihi Valley on Oahu, Hawaii. As well as the usual Zen practice of meditation, trainees practise Kyudo as a 'way of entering the realm of Zen consciousness'.

In Europe, the Zen master Taisen Deshimaru often worked in conjunction with senior martial arts sensei (teachers) to introduce Western martial artists to the great Zen traditions which underpinned the physical practice of their arts.

To bring this chapter to a close, here is a famous Japanese story which illustrates the profound influence that Zen has had on the martial arts.

Tsukuhara Bokuden was a great swordsman. He had three sons, all of whom were trained in the martial arts. He decided to test their proficiency and so placed a small cushion at the top of the entrance to his room, so arranged that anyone entering the room would cause it to fall.

He called in his first son. As he entered the room he noticed the cushion, reached up and removed it and bowed to his father. The second son was called. He dislodged the cushion, but caught it smoothly, bowed and replaced it. As the third son entered the room the cushion struck him on the head. He drew his sword and cut it in half before it hit the floor, smiling at his father in pride at his speed, accuracy and timing.

Bokuden told his sons to sit. To the first he said 'You are a skilful swordsman.'

To the second son he said, 'There is still more to learn, keep training.'

He then turned to his third son and said, 'You are a disgrace. You know nothing of the way of the sword. Train hard every day!'

10 · COMMON QUESTIONS

Most of us practising Zen have asked the following questions at some time in our training, either of ourselves or of a Zen teacher. There is no single right answer to any of them but to provide a general sense of the Zen response to such questions we have selected answers from a variety of contemporary Zen and other Buddhist teachers.

What is Enlightenment?

Enlightenment is only a name. If you make enlightenment, then enlightenment exists. But if enlightenment exists, ignorance exists too. Good and bad, right and wrong, enlightened and ignorant, all these are opposites. All opposites are just your own thinking. The truth is absolute, beyond thinking, beyond opposites. If you make something, you will get something. But if you don't make anything, you will get everything.

Is enlightenment really just a name? Doesn't a Zen master have to attain the experience of enlightenment in order to be a Zen master?
The Heart Sutra says that there is no attainment, with nothing to attain. If enlightenment is attained, it is not enlightenment.

Then everyone is enlightened?
Do you understand no-attainment?

No.
No-attainment is attainment. You must attain no-attainment! So what is attainment? What is there to attain?

104

Emptiness?
In true emptiness, there is no shame and no form. So there is no attainment. If you say 'I have attained true emptiness', you are wrong.
I'm beginning to understand. That is, I think I am.
The universe is always true emptiness. Now you are living in a dream. Wake up! Then you will understand.
How can I wake up?
I hit you! Very easy.
Would you please explain a bit more?
Okay. Can you see your eyes?
In a mirror.
That is not your eyes: it is only their reflection. Your eyes cannot see themselves. If you want to see your eyes, there is already a mistake. If you want to understand your mind, there is already a mistake.
But when you were a young monk, you had the actual experience of enlightenment. What was this experience?
I hit you.
(Silence)
Okay, suppose we have before us some honey, some sugar, and a banana. All are sweet. Can you explain the difference between honey's sweetness, sugar's sweetness, and banana's sweetness?
Hmmm.
But each is a different sweetness, yah? How can you explain to me?
I don't know.
But you could say, 'Open your mouth. This is honey, this is sugar, this is a banana'. So to understand your true self, you must understand the meaning of my hitting you. I have already put enlightenment into your mind.

From a conversation between Korean Zen Master Seung Sahn and a Zen student, see Zen, *Direct Pointing at Reality*; A. Bancroft, Thames & Hudson, 1979.

What do we experience in Enlightenment?

Even the term experience is not accurate, but for lack of better terminology we use the word experience. Actually there is no experience of enlightenment because there is no one there to experience it in that moment. It is actually the experience of no experience. All the time, every moment, we are experiencing all kinds of things through our senses: we are seeing things, we are hearing, smelling, touching, thinking, so forth. And we take for granted that there is an experiencer, the one who experiences all these things. Despite experiencing a constant bombardment of sensations, we are always looking for that one experience that is going to completely transform and change our life and give us eternal happiness, eternal bliss, eternal life, or whatever.

However, the very quest for that one experience keeps us divided and keeps us from experiencing reality as it is. It keeps us from experiencing what is actually happening in the moment because we are always waiting for that one great experience that is going to be the real thing. We are not really living and experiencing each moment. There is always that division between the experiencer and the experience, and the expectation of some other experience.

We have this expectation that there is going to be that great experience and we seek for and want to have it. We figure that this experience is going to resolve all our questions and we suffer a lot in our seeking for it. What actually happens is the very search itself creates our suffering and our confusion. We have a problem. We are seeking this experience called enlightenment and we believe this is going to really liberate us. That very seeking itself creates our anguish, our suffering. We expect that we are going to find something and thereby end our seeking. But it is actually the contrary. We have to give up the seeking first. Of course, someone can say to us, 'Just stop seeking, put an end to seeking.'

From a transcript of a talk given by Genpo Merzel Sensei, 1986.

Is Za-zen a Religion?

According to how you define religion, za-zen might be a religion or might not be. In many cases the word religion is used in the sense of a sect or creed. Za-zen is in no sense a sect or creed nor should it be.

Continuously from the primitive religions of ancient times, religion is concerned with man's relationship to an authority above him. People are put under a suggestive spell by the words of that authority, that is, the words of God, divine revelation, or mediums and representatives of God who have received the revelations, and call the absolute submission to this authority, 'religion'. Zen is not a religion in this sense either . . .

Zen Buddhism has inherited Shakyamuni's basic attitude towards life which is just to live out the life of the Self. Therefore, in Zen Buddhism, we just actualize within the Self the most refined attitude towards life. If religion means the teachings about the most refined attitude towards life, then Buddhism is certainly pure religion. But as I've already said, this Self is not simply the 'I' as opposed to other people and things. To live out the life of the 'Self' doesn't mean the self-intoxication of 'I' alone. Rather, this attitude towards life is to discover life which is pervading throughout all things within the Self. It is to live aiming at the manifestation of life in each and everything we meet and to see everything we meet as an extension of our own life. This attitude towards life is called compassion. A man who can't find compassion for others within the Self cannot be called a man of za-zen who has 'awakened' to the reality of the life of the Self.

Look at the following quotes from the Bible. 'God's will be done.' 'Whether therefore you eat, or drink, or whatever you do, do all to the glory of God.' 'Because God loves us, we know love. We express our love for God by loving others.'

This basic Christian attitude towards life is also the basic Buddhist attitude towards life.

Kosho Uchiyama Roshi, *Approach to Zen*, Japan Publications, Inc., 1973.

Can a Christian Practise Zen?

The truth of the matter is that you can hardly set Christianity and Zen side by side and compare them. This would almost be like trying to compare mathematics and tennis. However, when these traditions are understood in their pure state they can complement each other.

Thomas Merton, a Catholic monk who wrote about Zen.

Both St John and Meister Eckhart insist that the only way to union with God is through letting go of all images, thoughts and forms of God, and, furthermore, that such union is not a new situation but the discovery of that which has been from the very beginning.

For such Christians, awakening is proof of God's infinite mercy; for the Zen Buddhist, union with God is seeing into our true nature. However, there are Christians for whom the important fact is the uniqueness of Christ as the only true manifestation of God-as-man. And there are Zen Buddhists for whom what matters is that practice should be carried on according to a strict model and that rituals should all be unequivocally Buddhist. For these Christians and Zen Buddhists there can be no rapprochement. But in either case it is unwise to try to bring about a merging of Christianity and Buddhism; what is needed is to explore the ground that is neither Christian nor Buddhist.

We shall not cease from exploration,
And the end of all our exploring
Will be to arrive where we started
And know the place for the first time.

                              T.S. Eliot, *Four Quartets.*

Albert Low, *An Invitation to Practice Zen*, Charles E. Tuttle, 1989.

Isn't the Wish to Practise Za-zen a Desire?

There is no doubt that usually when people first decide to practise and do za-zen, they think that they will somehow improve themselves. As long as this is so, it is a desire. I call it a desire because these people, turning to the future and outside themselves, depict the goal of improving themselves and want to become that kind of self. However, this desire is to feel the value of life in the search for a goal (object) and so they are completely side-tracked from the manifestation of the raw life of the Self. Dogen Zenji says the following in the *Shobogenzo: Genjo Koan*: 'When a man first seeks the Dharma, he is far away from its environs.' But real improvement of the Self isn't to put aside this 'I' and chase after goals in the future, or outside ourselves, but it is to live the reality of the life of the Self here and now. When our attitude is thus changed, this is no longer desire. This is just the manifestation of your own life without turning towards goals outside yourself.

Then, what in the world do you call this power? You don't call it desire; it's the life force. When the living bodies of plants or animals are injured, they heal naturally. Grass by the roadside which is being crushed by a rock pushes out from the side of the rock and continues to grow. Do you suppose that the power to heal and the power to transcend obstacles is desire? Not at all. This is the life force. The power with which we do za-zen and practice is the same. Without having any goals or expectations, this power manifests and actualizes the reality of the life of the Self.

Kosho Uchiyama Roshi, *Approach to Zen*, Japan Publications, Inc., 1973.

One's initial approach to meditation is one that is earnestly looking for a rapid return on the investment of time and effort. How am I doing? Was that a good sign? How long does it take? I can't be trying hard enough.

What actually happens is that Buddhism slowly but surely turns the tables on you. As you get the feel for meditation, so you start to do it not to become a better person, not to get rid of anxiety, not to change at all, but to investigate what's so right here and now, in your experience. Discovering in microscopic detail who and what you are, moment to moment, becomes the focus of interest, and in doing so, the constant nagging feeling that 'This isn't it. There must be something better', falls away. The title of one of Milan Kundera's novels, *Life Is Elsewhere*, sums up our normal attitude; but in meditation you begin to grasp the trivially obvious, and utterly profound, fact that Life is Here Now.

Guy Claxton, *The Heart of Buddhism*, Crucible, 1990.

How can you Purify the Mind?

Hui-neng insisted that the whole idea of purifying the mind was irrelevant and confusing, because 'Our own nature is fundamentally clear and pure'. In other words, there is no analogy between consciousness or mind and a mirror that can be wiped. The true mind is 'no-mind' (Mu-hsin), which is to say that it is not to be regarded as an object of thought or action, as if it were a thing to be grasped and controlled. The attempt to work on one's own mind is a vicious circle. To try to purify it is to be contaminated with purity. Obviously this is the Taoist philosophy of naturalness, according to which a person is not genuinely free, detached, or pure when his state is the result of an artificial discipline. He is just imitating purity, just 'faking' clear awareness. hence the unpleasant self-righteousness of those who are deliberately and methodically religious.

Hui-neng's teaching is that instead of trying to purify or empty the mind, one must simply let go of the mind – because the mind is nothing to be grasped. Letting go of the mind is also equivalent to letting go of the series of thoughts and impressions (nien) which come and go 'in' the mind, neither repressing them, holding them, nor interfering with them.

Alan Watts, *The Way Of Zen*, Rider, 1987

Is it Wrong to Eat Meat?

There is fundamentally no birth and no death as we die and are born. When we kill the spirit that may realize this fact, we are violating this precept. We kill that spirit in ourselves and in others when we brutalize human potential, animal potential, earth potential. We brutalize with a casual word or a look sometimes; it does not take a club or a bomb.

War and other acts of organized violence, including social repression, are massive violations of this precept. It is ironic that sometimes one can be considerate of the feelings of friends and neighbours while working on a job that directly contributes to widespread suffering.

At the other end of the scale, we find Jain monks who filter their water in an attempt not to harm the microscopic creatures that inhabit it. Recent studies suggest that carrots and cabbages show responses to being cut or uprooted. What can we do? The answer is, I think, to eat and drink in the spirit of grateful sharing. I have heard that someone once asked Alan Watts why he was a vegetarian. He said: 'Because cows scream louder than carrots.' This reply may serve as a guideline. Some people will refuse to eat red meat. Some people will not drink milk. Some people will eat what is served to them, but will limit their own purchases of animal products. You must draw your own line, considering your health and the health of other beings.

Robert Aitkin, *Taking The Path Of Zen*, North Point Press, San Francisco, 1982.

Roshi: Meat eating, incidentally, is not specifically prohibited by the precepts. Nonetheless, the Lankavatara and Surangama sutras – both Mahayana scriptures – are quite eloquent in their condemnation of meat-eating.
Questioner: What reasons do they give?
Roshi: That there is not one being which, in its karmic evolution and devolution through countless rebirths, has not been our mother, our father, husband or wife, sister, brother, son or daughter – not one being whose kinship with us, even while living in the animal state, has not continued. How then can any spiritual person who approaches all living things as if they were himself eat the flesh of something that is of the same nature as himself? Seen this way, isn't all flesh-eating a form of cannibalism? How can anyone who seeks liberation from suffering inflict pain directly or indirectly on another creature? Those who eat the flesh of an animal obviously enjoy it, so in effect they are deriving pleasure from the death of another living being.

Roshi Philip Kapleau, *Zen Merging Of East And West*, Anchor Books, New York, 1980.

What is the Zen View on Sex and Chastity?

The mind – the universe-mind, which is the essential human mind – is pure, empty infinity. There is nothing to be called sexual exploitation there. We obscure this purity with clouds of covering and scheming. Sex is sharing, but when it becomes using, it is perverted – a violation not only of this precept, but of the earlier two precepts as well, for it involves brutalizing and taking things of others. Like the thief, the person who indulges in casual sex may be seeking to draw something from outside. Another kind of casual sex rises from a lack of confidence in the self as the agent of the Dharma, it is a kind of false-sharing, a prostitution.

People who have been conditioned by overliteral Catholic teaching or who have been followers of Yogananda or certain other Hindu teachers may come to Zen Buddhism with ideals of purity that interfere with the practice. The person for whom sexual purity is a psychological problem has little energy left over for za-zen. Sex is neither pure nor impure. Our attitude about it can be either disruptive or conducive to deep practice. If two people are committed to one another, their sexual fulfilment in each other can be a positive support to their za-zen.

Robert Aitken (discussing the third of the Ten Precepts, which he describes as No Misuse of Sex), *Taking the Path of Zen*, North Point Press, San Francisco, 1982.

What is the Place of Women in the Zen Tradition?

Another significant feature of Zen in the West is the full-fledged participation of women. In most Asian countries Buddhism perpetuated the sexist attitudes of the entire culture, and Zen was no exception. The spiritual lineage of Zen is called the 'patriarchal line'. Eisai, a twelfth-century Zen pioneer in Japan, stressed that 'nuns, women, or evil people should on no account be permitted to stay overnight' in a monastery. Only in recent years have Japanese Zen nuns been allowed to ordain disciples or serve as head priests of temples.

In contrast, women have been instrumental in North American (and European) Zen since its inception. Men and women sit shoulder to shoulder in the meditation hall, and women are in positions of influence at each of the major Zen centres. Members of the Diamond Sangha in Hawaii publish a journal about women and Zen called *Kahawai*. Several women have now become teachers themselves, consciously exploring ways to exercise spiritual authority without becoming authoritarian. For example, one female teacher eschews the traditional Zen warning stick and instead uses her hands to strike (or even massage) the shoulders of seated meditators.

Kenneth Kraft (Editor), *Zen Traditions And Transition*, Rider, 1988.

What is the Difference between Soto and Rinzai Zen?

The question of how za-zen and other forms of practice relate to enlightenment or Buddhahood is a fundamental issue that divides the Rinzai and Soto schools today. The Rinzai teaching is that supreme exertion is needed in order to awaken to the truth that all beings are essentially buddhas. This awakening is called 'seeing the nature' (Kensho) – that is, seeing Buddha-nature or one's Own Nature. Rinzai masters insist that koan practice is the most efficacious way to attain an initial kensho experience. Thereafter, they hold, one's insight should be deepened and refined by further koan study until the experience of enlightenment is fully integrated into one's being. The Soto position is that because all beings are essentially buddhas, enlightenment manifests itself in seated meditation right from the start, and it should not be conceived as something to be gained in practice. Soto teachers stress faith in one's original enlightenment, and they advocate an attitude of non-seeking as the proper frame of mind with which to practice Zen. By adhering to the rules of ritual propriety one is acting like what one already is – a buddha.

T. Griffith Foulk, Kenneth Kraft (Editors), *Zen Traditions and Transition*, Rider, 1988.

It is unfortunate that we in the West have inherited this opposition, which is essentially a Japanese problem. There is fundamentally no difference between these two Zen sects; there is just the question of emphasis. The Soto sect emphasizes the truth that we are already, as we are, here and now, fully awakened, whereas the Rinzai emphasizes the importance of knowing this existentially for ourselves. It is like the difference between someone who says, 'The taste of ice cream is great', and someone else who tastes it and says, 'Yes, it is'.

Albert Low, *An Invitation to Practice Zen*, Charles E. Tuttle, 1989.

How does Zen fit into the Mahayana Buddhist Tradition?

Although Zen in its basic tenets generally agrees with other schools of the Mahayana tradition, two characteristics are particularly marked in its teachings. First is the tendency to brush aside elaborate doctrinal theories and to urge the student to concentrate directly upon basic enlightenment experience. Secondly to demand that the student view enlightenment and its implications in terms of his own immediate situation.

The deliberate avoidance of technical religious terminology is a reflection of the Zen belief that one has not fully grasped the significance of enlightenment until one can manifest it in the language of daily life.

Burton Watson, *Zen Tradition and Transition* (Ed. Kenneth Kraft), Rider, 1988.

What is Ordinary Mind?

Sensei Genpo prefers to use the term 'natural mind' since in every day language 'ordinary' has connotations that are unsuitable. Ordinary mind in Zen refers to a mind that is involved in the ordinary world, moving as usual but not clinging to anything. Another sense of its meaning comes from the root meaning of the Chinese for ordinary mind, p'ing-ch'ang, used by Ma-tsu (AD 709–788), which suggests a mind that is level (p'ing) and constant (ch'ang), or in a state of constant equanimity. In either sense there is no attachment.

David Scott.

What is Karma?

Universal law of cause and effect, which according to the Buddhist view takes effect in the following way: 'The deed (karma) produces a fruit under certain circumstances; when it is ripe then it falls upon the one responsible. For a deed to produce this fruit, it must be morally good or bad, and be conditioned by a volitional impulse, which in that it leaves a trace in the psyche of the doer, leads his destiny in the direction determined by the effect of the deed. Since the time of ripening generally exceeds a lifespan, the effect of actions is necessarily one of more rebirths, which together constitute the cycle of existence.'

The Rider Encyclopedia of Eastern Philosophy and Religion, Rider, 1989.

All you can know is that what you've done in the past is a memory now. The most awful, disgusting thing that you've ever done . . . that is a memory, and that memory is the karmic result. The additions to that like fearing, worrying, speculating – these are the karmic result of unenlightened behaviour. What you do, you remember; it's as simple as that. If you do something kind, generous or compassionate, the memory makes you feel happy; and if you do something mean and nasty, you have to remember that. You try to repress it, run away from it, get caught up in all kinds of frantic behaviour – that's the karmic result.

Ajahn Sumedho quoted in *The Buddhist Handbook*, John Snelling, Century, 1987.

When we act or react from an underlying motive of meanness, defensiveness or acquisitiveness, there are always likely to be unfortunate repercussions. We don't perceive accurately. We create upset or anger in other people. We sabotage our own self-esteem, and store up bad memories in our minds. This is the heart of what Buddhism means by karma. It is useful to be clear about this, because karma is a notion that has been interpreted, especially by Westerners, in a variety of different ways, not all of them accurate. Often karma is taken to mean the results of our unenlightened actions, and in a sense this is true. As ye sow, so shall ye reap. But the results that are referred to are not forfeits doled out by a universe that has a sort of built-in system of retribution, but the everyday costs, in terms of the quality of relationships, and the degree of self-respect we feel, that naturally accrue.

Guy Claxton, *The Heart of Buddhism*, Crucible, 1990.

Is there Life after Death?

'No meaningful discussion of rebirth is possible without an understanding of karma.' Every intentional deed and thought of our past lives affects our present life, and our present voluntary deeds and thoughts will determine the nature of our future lives. To be free of the bondage of this cycle of birth-and-death is one of the chief objects of Buddhist practice. Karma, however, is not fatalism. Buddha condemned this idea. There is a fixed karma (such as being born a man instead of a woman) and there is a variable karma (such as the state of one's health over which one may exert control). It is always possible by one's own efforts to alter one's destiny to a limited extent.

The belief in survival and rebirth logically led to the doctrine that death is a transient state and not to be feared as a tragic end. It is inevitable, natural, and transitory. 'Life and death present the same cyclic continuity observed in all aspects of nature.'

Roshi Philip Kapleau, *Zen Merging of East and West*, Anchor Books, New York, 1980.

Opinions differ among Buddhist teachers as to whether belief in some kind of rebirth is required in order to be a Buddhist. Some, especially those who have come to the West from the East, are so used to thinking in terms of 'past lives' that it seems impossible to give it up. The Tibetan tradition, for example, places great store by the lineage of enlightened teachers, many of who are firmly believed to be the reincarnation of earlier masters. Others, however, are prepared to treat the idea of rebirth as a metaphor or a symbol, referring to the way in which an individual can be reborn into a new form of consciousness moment to moment, in just the same way that some Christian scholars see the resurrection of Christ as a powerful image rather than a necessary historical reality.

Guy Claxton, *The Heart of Buddhism*, Crucible, 1990.

What was the Beginning of the Universe?

We can think of ignorance as a beginning. When people asked the Buddha about the beginning of the universe, he never answered that question. That was one of the 'four imponderables' which he did not wish to elaborate on. He pointed to ignorance as the cause of our problems. When total liberation is reached one knows the answers to all the questions anyway and until then it is only necessary to practise to reach that state.

The other three imponderables are: 1. the intricacies of karma, 2. the range of influence of a Buddha, 3. the range of influence of a person in meditative absorption.

Anon.

What is Karma?

All the actions we take or thoughts we have, good or bad, affect how we feel about our lives and how other people respond towards us and they influence how we will continue to act and think. Like an oil painting the picture of our lives is built up of many differently coloured brush strokes only here each one represents a thought or action. The final portrait is our own responsibility and a perfect picture of our karmic state. To be free of karma is not to be free of the results of one's past actions but to be able to accept without discrimination one's individual destiny. If we can genuinely not judge the events in our lives as good or bad then karma ceases to have power.

David Scott.

11 · ZEN VOWS AND SUTRAS

Chanting vows and extracts from the sutras is an integral part of Zen practice. This chanting usually takes place after a period of za-zen. The chant is accompanied by the beating of a wooden drum (a mokugyo) and the striking of a gong (keisu). Here are some common Zen chants.

Verse of the Kesa
(after dawn za-zen)

Vast is the robe of liberation
A formless field of benefaction
I wear the Tathagata teaching
Saving all sentient beings

The Four Vows
(after evening za-zen)

Sentient beings are numberless,
I vow to save them;
Desires are inexhaustible,
I vow to put an end to them;
The Dharmas are boundless,
I vow to master them.

The Buddha Way is unsurpassable
I vow to attain it.

Gatha on Opening the Sutra
(before Teisho or Dharma talk)

The Dharma, incomparably profound and infinitely subtle,
is rarely encountered, even in millions of ages.
Now we see it, hear it, receive and maintain it;
May we completely realize the Tathagata's true meaning.

The Verse of Atonement

All evil karma committed by me since of old
On account of my beginningless greed, anger and ignorance
Born of my body, mouth and thought –
Now I atone for it all.

The Three Treasures

I take refuge in the Buddha
I take refuge in the Dharma
I take refuge in the Sangha

I take refuge in the Buddha,
The incomparably honoured one;
I take refuge in the Dharma,
honourable for its purity;
I take refuge in the Sangha,
honourable for its harmony.

I have taken refuge in the Buddha.
I have taken refuge in the Dharma.
I have taken refuge in the Sangha.

An Extract from the Shobogenzo Genjo Koan
by Dogen Zenji (1200–1253)

To study the Buddha Way is to study oneself.
To study oneself is to forget oneself.
To forget oneself is to be enlightened by the ten thousand
dharmas.

To be enlightened by the ten thousand dharmas is to be freed from one's body and mind and those of others.

No trace of enlightenment remains, and this traceless enlightenment is continued forever.

When first one seeks the Dharma, one is far away from its environs.

When one has already correctly transmitted the Dharma to oneself, one is one's original self at that moment.

When riding on a boat, if one watches the shore, one may assume that the shore is moving.

But watching the boat directly, one knows that it is the boat that moves.

If one examines the ten thousand dharmas with a deluded body and mind, one will suppose that one's mind and nature are permanent.

But if one practises intimately and returns to the true self, it will be clear that the ten thousand dharmas are without self.

Firewood turns into ash, and does not turn into firewood again.

But do not suppose that the ash is after and the firewood before.

We must realize that firewood is in the state of being firewood, and it has its before and after. Yet despite this past and future, its present is independent of them.

Ash is in the state of being ash, and it has its before and after.

Just as firewood does not become firewood again after it is ash, so after one's death, one does not return to life again.

Thus, that life does not become death is an unqualified fact of the Buddha-dharma; for this reason, life is called the non-born.

That death does not become life is the Buddha's revolving of the confirmed Dharma-wheel; therefore, death is called the non-extinguished.

Life is a period of itself.

Death is a period of itself.

Song of Za-Zen
A Poem by Hakuin Ekaku Zenji (1685–1768)

From the beginning all beings are buddha.
Like water and ice.
Without water and ice,

outside us no buddhas.
How near the truth
Yet how far we seek,
Like one in water crying 'I thirst!'
Like the son of a rich man wandering poor on this earth,
We endlessly circle the six worlds.
The cause of our sorrow is ego delusion.
From dark path to dark path we've wandered in darkness –
How can we be free from the wheel of samsara?
The gateway to freedom is za-zen samadhi;
Beyond exaltation, beyond all our praises,
The pure Mahayana.
Observing the precepts, repentance, and giving,
The countless good deeds, and the way of right living
All come from za-zen.
Thus one true samadhi extinguishes evils;
It purifies karma, dissolving obstructions.
Then where are the dark paths to lead us astray?
The pure lotus land is not far away.
Hearing this truth, heart humble and grateful,
To praise and embrace it, to practise its wisdom.
Brings unending blessings, brings mountains of merit
And if we turn inward and prove our True-nature,
That True self is no self,
Our own Self is no self –
We go beyond ego and past clever words.
Then the gate to the oneness of cause and effect
Is thrown open.
Not two and not three, straight ahead runs the Way.
Our form being no form,
In going and returning we never leave home.
Our thought now being no-thought,
Our dancing and songs are the voice of the dharma.
How vast is the heaven of boundless samadhi!
How bright and transparent the moonlight of wisdom!
What is there outside us,
What is there we lack?
Nirvana is openly shown to our eyes.
This earth where we stand is the Pure Lotus Land,
And this very body the body of buddha.

'Sandokai'
(Identity of Relative and Absolute)
By Sekito Kisen (AD 700–790)

The mind of the great sage of India was intimately conveyed from West to East. Among human beings are wise men and fools, but in the Way there is no northern or southern Patriarch. The subtle source is clear and bright; the tributary streams flow through the darkness. To be attached to things is illusion; to encounter the absolute is not yet enlightenment. Each and all, the subjective and objective spheres are related, and at the same time, independent. Related, yet working differently, though each keeps its own place. Form makes the character and appearance different; sounds distinguish comfort and discomfort. The dark makes all words one; the brightness distinguishes good and bad phrases. The four elements return to their nature as a child to its mother. Fire is hot, wind moves, water is wet, earth hard. Eyes see, ears hear, nose smells, tongue tastes the salt and sour. Each is independent of the other; cause and effect must return to the great reality. The words high and low are used relatively. Within light there is darkness, but do not try to understand that darkness; within darkness there is light, but do not look for that light. Light and darkness are a pair, like the foot before and the foot behind, in walking. Each thing has its own intrinsic value and is related to everything else in function and position. Ordinary life fits the absolute as a box and its lid. The absolute works together with the relative like two arrows meeting in mid-air. Reading words you should grasp the great reality. Do not judge by any standards. If you do not see the Way, you do not see it even as you walk on it. When you walk the Way, it is not near, it is not far. If you are deluded, you are mountains and rivers away from it. I respectfully say to those who wish to be enlightened:

Do not waste your time by night or day.

Maha Prajna Paramita Heart Sutra

'Prajna' is the Sanskrit word for wisdom or awareness without discrimination whilst 'paramita' means 'to cross to the other side'. This sutra propounds the case for 'prajna' as the route to a state beyond duality ('the other side').

The last line of this chant: Gate! Gate! Paragate! Parasamgate! Bodhi

Svana! means Gone! Gone! Gone Beyond! Gone Quite Beyond! Hail such an awakening!

AVALOKITESVARA Bodhisattva, doing deep prajna paramita,
Clearly saw emptiness of all five conditions,
Thus completely relieving misfortune and pain.
O Shariputra, form is no other than emptiness, emptiness no other than form;
Form is exactly emptiness, emptiness exactly form;
Sensation, conception, discrimination, awareness are likewise like this.
O Shariputra all dharmas are forms of emptiness, not born, not destroyed;
Not stained, not pure, without loss, without gain;
So in emptiness, there is no form, no sensation, conception discrimination, awareness;
No eye, ear, nose, tongue, body, mind;
No colour, sound, smell, taste, touch, phenomena;
No realm of sight . . . no realm of consciousness;
No ignorance and no end to ignorance . . .
No old age and death, and no end to old age and death;
No suffering, no cause of suffering, no extinguishing, no path;
No wisdom and no gain. No gain and thus
The bodhisvattva lives prajna paramita
With no hindrance in the mind, no hindrance, therefore no fear,
Far beyond deluded thoughts, this is nirvana.
All past, present and future Buddhas live prajna paramita, and therefore attain anuttara-samyak-sambodhi.
Therefore know, prajna paramita is the
The great Mantra, the vivid Mantra,
the best Mantra, the unsurpassable Mantra;
It completely clears all pain – this is the truth, not a lie.
So set forth the Prajna Paramita Mantra,
Set forth this mantra and say:
Gate! Gate! Paragate! Parasamgate!
Bodhi svaha! Prajna Heart Sutra.

GLOSSARY OF GENERAL TERMS

Anuttara-samyak-sambodhi All penetrating, perfect enlightenment.

Arhat One who is worthy and free from craving. This is the ideal of the Hinayana or Southern School of Buddhism.

Amitabha: The mythical Buddha of the Western Paradise much revered in the Judo Shien Shu sect of Japanese Buddhism on the basis that by his saving grace realization can be attained.

Avalokiteshvara The principal Bodhisattva in the Zen Buddhist tradition. Avalokiteshvara embodies boundless compassion for all sentient beings and is represented in male and female form. In Japan best known in female form, this Bodhisattva is called Kannon or Kanzeen.

Blue Cliff Record (Japanese **Hekiganroku**) A collection of one hundred koans compiled, with appreciatory verse, by Master Hsueh-tou Ch'ung-hsien (Jap. Setcho Juken, 980–1052) and with commentaries by Master Yuan-wu k'o-Ch'in (Jap. Ebgo Kokugon, 1063–1135).

Bodhi Sanskrit for enlightenment. Bodhi mind is an awakened mind.

Bodhidharma An Indian Buddhist who went to China and founded the Ch'an school (Zen in Japan) of Buddhism. The first Zen Patriarch.

Bodhisattva One who practises the Buddha way but who out of compassion for other sentient beings puts off his own enlightenment to help all to be free and awakened. This is the ideal of Mahayana, a Northern School of Buddhism of which Zen is a part.

Buddha Enlightened one. Shakyamuni Buddha refers to the historical Buddha, literally sage of the Shakya clan.

Buddha Way The path to enlightenment taught by the Buddha.

Butsu Japanese for Buddha.

Ch'an Chinese word for the Sanskrit word dhyana (meaning meditation). Name given to Chinese school of Buddhism founded by Bodhidharma. Translated into Japanese becomes Zen.

Dharma Sanskrit word meaning The Law. Used in a variety of ways. May mean the teachings of the Buddha, the whole body of Buddhist literature, universal truth, self nature, or just 'the way'.

Dhyana *See* Ch'an.

Diamond Sutra A portion of the Prajna Paramita Sutra much valued in the Zen tradition.

Dogen A great figure in the history of Zen. Born in Japan in 1200, Dogen founded the Japanese Soto school of Zen. He is the author of *Shobogenzo*, which means The Eye of The True Law, an important collection of Dharma essays.

Dukkha The First Noble Truth taught by the Buddha. Translated as 'suffering' dukkha is said to originate from desire. (*See* **Four Noble Truths**.) Dukkha may also be understood as the underlying unsatisfactoriness of life experienced by most people.

Eightfold Path The path leads to liberation, consisting of right understanding, right aim, right speech, right action, right livelihood, right effort, right mindfulness, and right concentration.

Enlightenment (also **Satori**) The direct experience and realization of one's true nature (also called one's Buddha nature).

Four Noble Truths Fundamental teaching of the Buddha concerning human life. They are:

1. life is suffering (dukkha);
2. suffering has a cause;
3. there is a way to put an end to the cause of suffering;
4. the way to put an end to the cause of suffering is the Eightfold Path.

Gateless Gate A collection of forty-eight koans compiled, with commentary and appreciatory verse, by Wu-men Hu-k'ai (Jap. Mumon Ekai) in the thirteenth century.

Heart Sutra A condensed version of the Prajna Paramita Sutra highlighting the most important teachings.

Jukai Buddhist ceremony in which the Zen student makes a commitment to maintain the precepts.

Kensho Literally means seeing into one's nature; it is the experience of satori.

Koan Originally it meant a public case which established a legal precedent. In Zen it is an apparently paradoxical story assigned to a student to solve, in order to help their awakening or to test the deepness of their realization. There are about 1700 recorded koans (pronounced in Japanese ko-an). Notable collections may be found in the Mumonkan (The Gateless Gate) and the Hekiganroku (The Blue Cliff Record).

Mu As used in the koan 'Joshua's Dog' (Chao-chou (778–897) when asked by a monk, 'Does a dog have Buddha nature?' replied, 'Mu!') It is a meaningless exclamation pointing directly at Reality. Often the first koan given to a Zen student.

Paramitas The six perfections practised by Bodhisattvas. The paramitas include wisdom (prajna), patience (kshanti), generosity (dana), meditative awareness (dhyana), effort (virya) and precepts (sila).

Prajna Wisdom in which discriminating consciousness and all dualism have been transcended.

Precepts The sixteen precepts are: the Three Treasures (be one with the Buddha, be one with the Dharma, be one with the Sangha), the Three Pure Precepts (do not commit evil, do good, do good for others), the Ten Grave Precepts (do not kill, do not steal, do not be greedy, do not lie, do not be ignorant, do not talk about others' faults, do not elevate yourself by criticizing others, do not be stingy, do not get angry, do not speak ill of the Three Treasures).

Samadhi One pointed non-dualistic awareness.

Satori Enlightenment. The experience of realizing one's true nature.

Sangha Buddhist priesthood or monastic order or simply a community of Buddhists. Also implies the harmonious relationship of all sentient beings.

Sesshin A Zen retreat, a period of intensive Zen practice. Usually seven days long.

Shikantaza Just to sit. Za-zen without the exercises or breath counting or koan study.

Sutra Buddhist scriptures or texts recording works attributed directly to the Buddha or to other enlightened Buddhist teachers.

Za-zen Seated meditation. In Zen, za-zen is also used to describe generally the exercises of breath counting, shikantaza and koan study practised while in the za-zen position.

MONASTIC OR
SESSHIN GLOSSARY

Ango Three months intensive training period.
Daisan Interviews with Zen instructor.
Dennan Altar attendant; distributes sutra books.
Densho Large hanging bell which announces services.
Doan Person who hits bell and gongs during service.
Dokusan Interviews with Roshi.
Fusatsu Renewal of vows ceremony.
Fushinzamu Community work.
Gaitan Front and back porches.
Han Hanging wooden block, struck to announce za-zen period.
Hosan Days off.
Ino Head leader of chanting.
Jijo Officiant of services attendant, carries the incense box.
Jikido Officient responsible for monastic schedule and keeping time during za-zen.
Jisha Officiant or teacher's attendant.
Jukai Taking of the precepts.
Junko Walking with the Awakening stick.
Kinhin Walking meditation.
Kyosaku Awakening stick.
Mokugyo Wooden fish – wood drum that keeps beat during services.
Nenju Formal thanksgiving to Roshi in the Zendo.
Oryoki Formal meals, eating out of three bowls.

Roshi Head teacher, Zen Master.
Samu Work.
Sensei Certified teacher.
Shuso Head training monk for three month period.
Shuso Hossen Ceremony of testing Shuso's understanding.
Tan Woven rice straw mats.
Tenzo Head cook.
Zabutan Square sitting mats.
Zafu Round sitting cushions.
Zendo Main meditation hall.

FURTHER READING

This is a very selective list of books that will give you a broad introduction to the history of Buddhism and Zen from the time of the Buddha to the present day. Many of the books listed contain their own comprehensive reading and source book bibliographies. Thus if you wish to delve further into a particular subject choose a title from the list here that covers the general area of interest and consult it for further titles of a more specific nature.

Aitken, R. *Taking The Path of Zen*, North Point Press, 1982.

Bancroft, A. *Zen, Direct Pointing at Reality*, Thames & Hudson, 1979.

Blofeld, J. *The Wheel of Life*, Rider, 1959.

Blofeld, J. *The Zen Teaching of Huang Po*, The Buddhist Society, 1968–1985.

Blyth, R.H. *Zen and the Zen Classics*, Hokuseido Press, Tokyo, 1962.

Carrithers, M. *The Buddha*, Oxford University Press, 1983.

Claxton, G. (Editor), *Beyond Therapy*, Wisdom, 1986.

Claxton, G. *The Heart of Buddhism*, Crucible, 1990.

Cleary, T. *The Inner Teachings of Taoism*, Shambhala.

Crook, J. and Fontana, D. (Editors), *Space in Mind*, Element Books, 1990.

Dumoulin, H. *A History of Zen Buddhism*, Faber & Faber, 1968.

Dumoulin, H. *Zen Enlightenment*, Weatherhill, 1979.

Eppstein F. (Editor), *The Path of Compassion*, Parallax Press, 1988.

Fromm, E. and Suzuki, D.T. *Zen Buddhism and Pyschoanalysis*, Souvenir Press, 1974.

Fung Yu Lan, *The Spirit of Chinese Philosophy*, R.K.P., 1962.

Harding, D. *On Having No Head*, R.K.P., 1986.

Humphries, C. *Sixty Years of Buddhism in England*, The Buddhist Society, London 1968.

Humphries, C. *Zen Buddhism*, Heinemann, 1949.

Kapleau, P. *The Buddhist Case For Vegetarianism*, Rider, 1982.

Kapleau, P. *Zen Merging of East and West*, Anchor Books, 1980.

Kapleau, P. *The Three Pillars of Zen*, Rider, 1980.

Katz N. (editor), *Buddhist and Western Psychology*, Shambhala, 1983.

Kraft, K. (Editor), *Zen Traditions and Transition*, Rider, 1988.

Legget, T. *A First Zen Reader*, Tuttle, Tokyo, 1960.

Legget, T. *Zen and the Ways*, R.K.P., 1978.

Linssen, R. *Zen, The Art of Life*, Pyramid, 1969.

Liu I-Ming (transl. T. Cleary), *Awakening To The Tao*, Shambhala, 1989.

Loori, J. D. *Mountain Record of Zen Talks*, Shambhala, 1988.

Low, A. *An Invitation to Practice Zen*, Charles E. Tuttle, 1989.

Luk, C. *Chan and Zen Teaching Vols 1–3*, Shambhala, 1987.

Merzel, D.G. *The Eye Never Sleeps (Striking to the Heart of Zen)*, Shambhala, 1991.

Price A.F. and Wong Mou-Lan (translators), *The Diamond Sutra and the Sutra of Hui Neng*, Shambhala, 1969.

Rahula, W. *What the Buddha Taught*, Gordon Fraser, 1972.

Roshi, K.U. *Approach to Zen*, Japan Publications Inc., 1973.

Schloegl, I. *The Zen Way*, Sheldon Press, 1977.

Sekida, K. *Zen Training*, Weatherhill, 1975.

Suzuki, D.T. *An Introduction to Zen Buddhism*, Rider, 1969.

Suzuki, D.T. *Manual of Zen Buddhism*, Rider, 1950.

Suzuki, D.T. *Zen and Japanese Culture*, Princeton University Press, 1970.

Suzuki, S. *Zen Mind Beginners' Mind*, Weatherhill, 1970.

Thomas, E.J. *The Life of the Buddha*, Kegan Paul, 1949.

Trungpa, C. *Cutting Through Spiritual Materialism*, Shambhala, 1973.

Watts, A.W. *The Way of Zen*, Thames & Hudson, 1960.

Welwood J. (editor), *The Awakening of the Heart*, Shambhala, 1983.

Wilber, K. *No Boundary (Eastern and Western Approaches to Personal Growth)*, Shambhala, 1981.

Wilber, K. *Up From Eden*, R.K.P., 1983.

READING LIST FOR ZEN AND THE MARTIAL ARTS

For those readers who may wish to look at the relationship between Zen and the martial arts in depth the following works are recommended:

Deshimaru, T. *The Zen Way to the Martial Arts*, Rider & Co., 1983.
Graf von Durkheim, K. *Hara The Vital Centre of Man*, Mandla, 1977.
——*The Japanese Cult of Tranquility*, Rider & Co., 1974.

Harris, V. *A Book of Five Rings*, Allison & Busby Ltd., 1974.
Herrigel, E. *Zen in the Art of Archery*, Routledge & Kegan Paul, 1978.
Kammer, R. *Zen and Confucius in the Art of Swordsmanship*, Routledge & Kegan Paul, 1978.
Kauz, H. *The Martial Spirit*, Overlook Press, 1977.
Kushner, K. *One Arrow, One Life*, Arkana, 1988.
Leggett, T. *A First Zen Reader*, Tuttle, 1975.
——*Encounters in Yoga and Zen*, Routledge & Kegan Paul, 1982.
——*The Warrior Koans*, Arkana, 1985.
——*Zen and the Ways*, Routledge & Kegan Paul, 1978.

Morisawa, J.S. *The Secret of the Target*, Routledge & Kegan Paul, 1988.
Nakamura, T. *Karate Technique and Spirit*, Shufunotomo Co. Ltd., Tokyo, 1986.
Newman, J. *Bushido The Way of the Warrior*, Magna Books, 1989.
Nukamya, K. *The Religion of the Samurai*, first published 1913, reprinted by Luzac & Co., 1973.
Scott Wilson, W. (trans) *The Unfettered Mind-Takuan Soho*, Kodansha International, 1986.
Sollier, A. and Gyorbiro, Z. *Japanese Archery: Zen in Action*, Weatherhill, 1969.
Stein, H.J. *Kyudo: The Art of Zen Archery*, Element Books, 1988.
Stevens, J. *The Sword of No Sword*, Shambala, 1984.
Suzuki, D.T. *Zen and Japanese Culture*, Princeton University Press, 1973.
Warner, G. and Draeger, D. F. *Japanese Swordsmanship*, Weatherhill, 1982.

CONTACT ADDRESSES

Rinzai Zen

London Zen Society
10 Belmont St., London NW1 8HH, UK. tel. 071–485 9576

Zen Studies Society (Eido Tai Shimano Rōshi)
New York Zendo Sobo-ji, 223 East 67th St., New York, NY 12758,
USA

Soto-Rinzai Tradition

Kanzeon Sangha/Zen Practice Centre Trust
14 Monkswell Rd., Exeter EX4 7AX.
(David Scott may be contacted at 21 Aigburth Drive, Liverpool,
L17 4JQ.)

Kanzeon Sangha (USA)
16140 S.W. Lindsay Court, Lake Oswego, OR 97035 USA.
tel. (503) 697 1856

Zen Center of Los Angeles (Taizen Maezumi Rōshi)
905 South Normandie Avenue, Los Angeles, CA 90006, USA

The Zen Center (Philip Kapleau Rōshi)
7 Arnold Park, Rochester, New York 14607, USA

Diamond Sangha (Robert Aitken Rōshi)
Koko-an Zendo, 2119 Kaloa Way, Honolulu, Hawaii 96822, USA

John Daido Loori, Zen Mountain Monastery, PO Box 197DC, Mt
Tremper, NY 12457, USA

Sōtō Zen

(Order of Buddhist Contemplatives – founded by Jiyu Kennett Rōshi)
Throssel Hole Priory, Carr Shield, nr Hexham, Northumberland NE47
8AL, UK. tel. 04985 204 (9.30 am – 7.00 pm)

L'Association Zen d'Europe (founded by Deshimaru Rōshi):
17 rue des Cinq-Diamants, F–75013 Paris, France

International Zen Association, UK
Nancy Amphoux, 21 Richmond Dale, Bristol

Zen Center of San Francisco (founded by Shunryū Suzuki)
300 Page St., San Francisco, CA 94012, USA

Chinese Zen (Ch'an)

Ch'an Retreats/Norwich Ch'an Ass'n (Richard Hunn)
20 St. Leonard's Rd., Thorpe Hamlet, Norwich, Norfolk NR1 4BL, UK

Dharma Realm Buddhist Association (Master Hsüan Hua
Gold Mountain Monastery, 1731 15th Street, San Francisco, CA
94103, USA

John Crook
Winterhead Farm, Shipham, Winscombe, Avon

Korean Zen

Stephen & Martine Batchelor
Sharpham North, Ashprington, Totnes, S. Devon TR9 7UT, UK

Bulsung Sa (founded by Kusan Sunim)
8 rue des Astres, CH–1200 Genève, Switzerland

Kwan Um Zen School (Seung Sahn Sunim)
Providence Zen Center, 528 Pound Rd., Cumberland, R.I. 02864, USA

Zen Lotus Society (Samu Sunim)
46 Gwynne Ave., Toronto, Ontario M6K 2C3, Canada

General Information

The Buddhist Society, 58 Eccleston Sq. London SW1V 1PH. tel.
071–834 5858

Also see *The Buddhist Directory* pub. by The Buddhist Society for
addresses in the UK and Ireland

and *The International Buddhist Directory* pub. Wisdom Press (23
Dering St., London W1. tel. 071–520 5588)

Sources List

Name	Dates	Important Writings	Role
Sengstan (Japanese Sosan)	died 606	Hsin Hsin Ming	Third Patriarch of Chinese Zen
Daiken Eno (Chinese Hui Neng)	638–713	Sutra of Hui Neng	6th Patriach of Chinese Zen
Nansen	748–834		
Rinzai Gigen (Chinese Lin Chin)	died 867	collected sayings	Great masters of Golden Age of Zen in China 620–906
Joshu Jushin	778–897		
Umon Bun'en	died 949		
Mumon Ekai	1183–1260	Mumonkan (Gateless Gate Koan collection)	Commentator and compiler of one of the most used koan collections
Eisai	1141–1215		Introduced Rinzai Zen to Japan
Eihei Dogen Kigen	1200–53	Shobogenzo and associated writings	Founder of Japanese Soto Zen
Bankei Yotaku	1622–93	Recorded talks	Important for originality of his teachings
Ekaku Hakuin	1686–1769	Za-zen Wasan (Song of Za-zen) and other writings	Reformed and revitalized Japanese Rinzai Zen
Daiun Sokaku Harada	1870–1961	Recorded talks	Soto master who went on to train under a great Rinzai teacher, Dokutan Roshi. Teacher to Yasutani Roshi (see below)

Name	Dates	Important Writings	Role
D T Suzuki	1870–1966	Essays in Zen Buddhism (3 vols) and numerous other works	Scholar, teacher and writer whose books on Zen were the first to be widely available in the West
Nyogen Senzaki	1876–1958	Recorded talks	One of the first teachers of Zen to become resident in the West
Kodo Sawaki	1880–1965	Recorded talks	Prominent Soto Zen Master. Teacher to Deshimaru Roshi (see below)
Hakuin Ryoko Yasutani	1885–1973	Recorded talks, see especially 'The Three Pillars of Zen' by Kapleau Roshi (see below)	Teacher to many modern Western and Japanese Zen Masters (including Maezumi, Kapleau and Aitken Roshis)
Christmas Humphreys	1901–83	Many books on Buddhism and Zen	Founder of the British Buddhist Society
Shunryn Suzuki	1905–71	Zen Mind, Beginners Mind	Founder of Zen Center of San Francisco
Taizen Deshimaru	1914–82	Questions to a Zen Master, The Ring of The Way, The Zen Way to the Martial Arts	Founder of French-based Soto School: International Zen Association
Alan Watts	1915–73	The Way of Zen and other works	Popularized Zen in the West
Myoko-ni		The Zen Way and other works	Zen teacher to British Buddhist Society
Hakuya Taizan Maezumi		On Zen Practice (3 vols) (with Bernard Tetsugen Glassmann Sensei)	Founder of Zen Center of Los Angeles
Jiyu Kennet		Zen is Eternal Life and other works	Founder of Soto Zen Order of Buddhist Contemplatives based at Mount Shastra, California, USA and Throssel Hole, Northumberland, UK

Name	Dates	Important Writings	Role
Robert Aitken		Taking the Path of Zen, The Mind of Clover and other works	Teacher to the Daimond Sangha (Hawaii)
Philip Kapleau		The Three Pillars of Zen, Zen Dawn in the West, To Cherish All Life	Founder of Zen Center of Rochester (USA)
Dennis Genpo Merzel		The Eye Never Sleeps	Teacher to Kanzeon Sangha (Europe and North America)
Albert Low		An Invitation to Practice Zen	Dharma successor to Philip Kapleau

INDEX